Brad Miser

Sams **Teach Yourself**

iCloud

in **10 Minutes**

SAMS | 800 East 96th Street, Indianapolis, Indiana 46240

Sams Teach Yourself iCloud in 10 Minutes

Copyright © 2012 by Sams Publishing

Library of Congress Cataloging-in-Publication Data
Miser, Brad.
  Sams teach yourself iCloud in 10 minutes / Brad Miser.
    p. cm.
  ISBN-13: 978-0-672-33596-9
  ISBN-10: 0-672-33596-4
  1. Cloud computing. 2. iCloud. 3. iPod (Digital music player)
  4. iPhone (Smartphone) 5. iOS (Electronic resource) I. Title.
  QA76.585.M57 2012
  004.6782–dc23

                                        2012002304

Printed in the United States of America

Second Printing: April 2012

Trademarks

All terms mentioned in this book that are known to be trademarks or service marks have been appropriately capitalized. Pearson cannot attest to the accuracy of this information. Use of a term in this book should not be regarded as affecting the validity of any trademark or service mark.

Warning and Disclaimer

Every effort has been made to make this book as complete and as accurate as possible, but no warranty or fitness is implied. The information provided is on an "as is" basis. The author and the information contained in this book.

Bulk Sales

Pearson offers excellent discounts on this book when ordered in quantity for bulk purchases or special sales. For more information, please contact

U.S. Corporate and Government Sales
1-800-382-3419
corpsales@pearsontechgroup.com

For sales outside of the U.S., please contact

International Sales
international@pearsoned.com

ISBN-10: 0-67-23359-64
ISBN-13: 978-0-67-23359-69

Editor-in-Chief
Greg Wiegand

Sr. Acquisitions Editor
Laura Norman

Development Editor
Lora Braughey

Technical Editor
Greg Kettell

Managing Editor
Kristy Hart

Project Editor
Anne Goebel

Copy Editor
Chrissy White

Senior Indexer
Cheryl Lenser

Proofreader
Sheri Cain

Compositor
Nonie Ratcliff

Book Designer
Gary Adair

Contents

About the Author

Brad Miser has written extensively about technology, with his favorite topics being Apple's amazing "i" technology, including iPods, iPhones, and now iCloud. Books Brad has written include *Sams Teach Yourself Mac OS X in 10 Minutes*; *Sams Teach Yourself iTunes 10 in 10 Minutes*; *My iPod touch, 3rd Ed*; *My iPhone, 5th Ed*; *Absolute Beginner's Guide to Homeschooling*; and *MacBook Pro Portable Genius, 3rd Ed*. He has also been an author, development editor, or technical editor on more than 50 other titles.

Brad is or has been a sales support specialist, the director of product and customer services, and the manager of education and support services for several software development companies. Previously, he was the lead proposal specialist for an aircraft engine manufacturer, a development editor for a computer book publisher, and a civilian aviation test officer/engineer for the U.S. Army. Brad holds a Bachelor of Science degree in mechanical engineering from California Polytechnic State University at San Luis Obispo and has received advanced education in maintainability engineering, business, and other topics.

Originally from California, Brad now lives in Brownsburg, Indiana, with his wife Amy; their three daughters, Jill, Emily, and Grace; a rabbit; and a sometimes-inside cat.

Brad would love to hear about your experiences with this book (the good, the bad, and the ugly). You can write to him at bradmiser@me.com.

Dedication

To those who have given the last full measure of devotion so the rest of us can be free.

Acknowledgments

A special thanks to Laura Norman, Acquisitions Editor extraordinaire, for involving me in this project. I appreciate the efforts of Lora Braughey, Development Editor, for ensuring the content of this book is meaningful and does allow you to learn iCloud in 10 minutes. Thanks to Greg Kettell, the Technical Editor, who made sure this book is accurate and "tells it like it is." Chrissy White deserves special mention for transforming my gibberish into readable text. And Kristy Hart and Anne Goebel deserve kudos for the difficult task of coordinating all the many pieces, people, and processes that are required to make a book happen. Last, but certainly not least, to the rest of the important folks on the team, including Cheryl Lenser, Cindy Teeters, Sheri Cain, Gary Adair, Nonie Ratcliff, and the rest of the top-notch Sams staff, I offer a sincere thank you for all of your excellent work on this project.

We Want to Hear from You

As the reader of this book, you are our most important critic and commentator. We value your opinion and want to know what we're doing right, what we could do better, what areas you'd like to see us publish in, and any other words of wisdom you're willing to pass our way.

You can email or write me directly to let me know what you did or didn't like about this book—as well as what we can do to make our books stronger.

Please note that I cannot help you with technical problems related to the topic of this book, and that due to the high volume of mail I receive, I might not be able to reply to every message.

When you write, please be sure to include this book's title and author, as well as your name and contact information. I will carefully review your comments and share them with the author and editors who worked on the book.

Email: consumer@samspublishing.com

Mail: Greg Wiegand
           Editor-in-Chief
           Sams Publishing
           800 East 96th Street
           Indianapolis, IN 46240 USA

Introduction

We all live in a connected world and most of us use multiple devices, such as iPhones, iPads, Macintosh computers, and Windows PCs. Using all of these devices for similar functions, such as email or working on documents, presents the challenge of keeping all our devices in sync so that we have the same information, such as calendars and emails, available to us no matter which device we happen to be using at any point in time.

Enter iCloud.

Apple's iCloud service provides an Internet "cloud" on which you can store all sorts of information and documents. Each of your devices can then connect to the cloud through the syncing process so they all have access to the same information and documents. The "flow" of information goes both ways, too; changes you make on a synced device move to the cloud to update its information (which in turn is communicated to the other synced devices).

iCloud enables you to manage and sync all sorts of information and documents. It helps with your music, books, apps, and TV shows, too, since the content you purchase from the iTunes Store is automatically downloaded to all your devices and is retrievable whether you are using an iOS device or a computer. And, with the optional iTunes Match service, all the music in your iTunes Library is available to any of your iOS devices from the cloud—no syncing required.

iCloud is a great extension of your digital self onto the Internet. It makes all your devices much more effective, and even more fun, to use.

About This Book

Similar to the other books in the *Sams Teach Yourself in 10 Minutes* series, the purpose of this book is to enable you to learn how to use iCloud quickly and easily; and, hopefully, you'll even enjoy yourself along the way! This book is composed of a series of lessons; and each lesson covers a specific topic related to the use of iCloud. For example, Lesson 2, "Configuring iCloud on an iPhone, iPod touch, or iPad," teaches you how to set up iCloud on iOS devices, while Lesson 11, "Using iCloud with Your Calendars," shows you how to take advantage of iCloud to help you manage your calendars.

The lessons generally build on each other, starting with the more fundamental topics covered in the earlier lessons and moving toward more advanced topics in the later lessons. In general, if you work from the front of the book toward the back, your iCloud education progresses smoothly. You need to start with Lesson 1, "Getting Started with Your iCloud Account and Website," to establish your iCloud base. From there, move onto the lessons that explain how to set up iCloud on the devices you use. Lesson 3, "Configuring iCloud on Macintosh Computers," explains how to set up iCloud on a Mac; and Lesson 4, "Configuring iCloud on Windows Computers," explains how to do the same on a Windows PC. After you have those bases covered, you can jump to the other lessons based on your areas of interest.

The lessons include both information and explanations along with step-by-step tasks. You get more out of the lessons if you perform the steps as you read the lessons. Figures are included to show you what key steps look like on your devices' screens.

Who This Book Is For

This book is for anyone who wants to get the most out of iCloud. While iCloud is well designed and relatively easy to use, you learn faster with this guide to help you. If you've never used iCloud, this book gets you started and helps you move toward becoming an iCloud guru. If you've previously dabbled with iCloud, this book helps you go beyond basic tasks and prepares you to use all of iCloud's amazing functionality. If you've spent a fair amount of time using iCloud, this book provides lessons to round out your iCloud expertise.

What Do I Need to Use This Book?

To make use of the information in this book, you need an iCloud account. Lesson 1 teaches you to create your own free account. You also need at least one device that can access iCloud; this can be an iOS device (iPhone, iPad, or iPod touch), a Mac, or a Windows PC. Your experience improves if you have more than one device, such as an iPad and a computer. If you are lucky enough to have more than two devices, even better!

In addition to the technical requirements, you just need a sense of adventure and curiosity to explore all this book offers you. iCloud is fun to use and, with this guide to help you, it should be fun to learn as well.

Conventions Used in This Book

Whenever you need to click a particular button or link or make a menu selection, you see the name of that item in **bold**, such as in "Click the **Save** button to save your document." You also find three special elements (Notes, Tips, and Cautions) throughout this book.

> NOTE: A note provides information that adds to the knowledge you gain through each lesson's text and figures.

> TIP: Tips offer alternate ways to do something, such as keyboard shortcuts, or point out additional features of which you can take advantage.

> CAUTION: You won't find many of these in this book, but when you do come across one, you should carefully read it to avoid problems or situations that could cause you grief, time, or money.

LESSON 1

Getting Started with Your iCloud Account and Website

In this lesson, you get an overview of iCloud, learn how to obtain an account, and how to use your iCloud website.

Understanding iCloud

iCloud is a service that connects your iOS devices, Macintosh computers, Windows computers, and Apple TVs to a "cloud," which is a central repository for data storage that is available via the Internet. Each device stores data on the cloud and receives data from the cloud. In this way, all your devices can share the same information.

> **NOTE: iOS Device**
>
> An iOS device runs Apple's iOS operating system software. An iOS device is an iPhone, iPod touch, or iPad. iCloud works very similarly on all these devices, which is why they are referred to together as iOS devices. When there are differences between them, you'll see them spelled out. (In the context of iCloud, there aren't many differences.)

The iCloud service manages the flow of data to and from each device through the syncing process, which happens automatically if your devices are configured to allow it.

The result is that you have the ability to access the same information from each device. For example, when you create a contact on an iPhone, that contact is stored on the iPhone and is also copied up to the cloud. From there, the contact is copied down to each device with which your iCloud account's contact information is synced, as shown in Figure 1.1. This ensures you have access to your contact information on each of your devices.

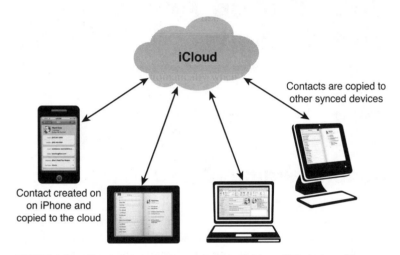

FIGURE 1.1   iCloud makes the same data available to iOS devices, Macs, and Windows PCs through the sync process.

In a similar way, iCloud can help you keep the following types of information in sync:

▶ Music, apps, and books that you purchase in the iTunes Store

▶ All the music in your iTunes Library (via the optional iTunes Match service)

▶ Photos (via Photo Stream)

▶ Documents

▶ Email

▶ Contacts

▶ Calendars

▶ Other information, such as bookmarks and notes

> NOTE: **Documents**
>
> As explained in Lesson 8, "Using iCloud with Your Documents," iCloud only supports documents associated with specific applications. For example, when this was written, iCloud document syncing worked natively within Pages, Numbers, and Keynote. You can use other applications, such as Word, with the downloaded versions of some documents (such as those from Pages). Over time, other developers will add iCloud support for their applications so you will be able to use iCloud for your documents more broadly.

You can also use iCloud to help locate and protect your iOS devices and Mac computers through the Find My iPhone/iPod/iPad/Mac application. In addition to locating a device, you can lock devices or even remotely wipe their memories if you've lost control of them.

Another useful function of iCloud is the ability to back up your iOS devices so that you can restore them in case something happens to them.

And if that isn't enough for you, you also get access to your own iCloud website that has web applications you can use along with tools with which you can manage your iCloud account.

To use iCloud, you first need to accomplish the following two tasks:

1. Obtain an iCloud account. This is explained in the next section.

2. Configure each device to use your iCloud account. This means that you log into your iCloud account and determine which type of information will be synced on the device. This task is explained in Lesson 2, "Configuring iCloud on an iPhone, iPod touch, or iPad," Lesson 3, "Configuring iCloud on Macintosh Computers," and Lesson 4, "Configuring iCloud on Windows Computers."

After iCloud is set up on each device, you can start working with the various services it provides. Each of these is explained in a later lesson in this book. For example, you can learn how to use iCloud for email in Lesson 9, "Configuring Your iCloud Email."

You don't have to use all of the iCloud services, nor do you have to start using them all at the same time. You can pick and choose which services you want to use and when you want to use them. And not all devices support all services. For example, you can't use contacts or calendar syncing with an Apple TV because it doesn't offer tools to work with that kind of information.

The devices that work with iCloud are the following:

▶ **iOS 5 devices.** Any iPhone, iPod touch, or iPad running iOS 5 or later are fully iCloud-compatible.

▶ **Macintosh computers.** To use iCloud on a Mac, you must be running Mac OS X Lion, version 10.7.2 or later, along with iTunes 10.5 or later. If you want to use Photo Stream, you need to have iPhoto'11, version 9.2 or later, or Aperture, version 3.2 or later.

▶ **Windows computers.** iCloud works with Microsoft Windows 7 or Vista running Service Pack 2 or later. You also need to install the iCloud control panel and have iTunes 10.5 installed. To have your calendars and contacts synced via iCloud, you need to have Outlook 2007 or 2010 installed. To sync your bookmarks, you need to have either Safari version 5.1.1 or later or Internet Explorer 8 or later. (Instructions to install the iCloud control panel are provided in Lesson 4.)

▶ **Apple TV.** iCloud can be used with an Apple TV running software version 4.4 or later.

NOTE: **Taming the Lion**

If you want to learn more about Lion, check out my book *Sams Teach Yourself Mac OS X Lion in 10 Minutes*.

Obtaining an iCloud Account

To use iCloud, you need an iCloud account. The good news is that you may already have one. The even better news is that an iCloud account is free to obtain and use. A free account includes access to almost all the services described in the previous section along with 5GB of online storage space.

> NOTE: **iCloud Is Mostly Free**
>
> To use iTunes Match, an annual fee is required. Also, if you want to increase your online disk space, you need to pay an annual fee. (Managing your online disk space is explained later in this book.)

If you have any of the following accounts, you already have an iCloud account and are ready to start using iCloud:

▶ **Apple Online Store and iTunes Store.** If you've ever shopped at the online Apple Store or the iTunes Store, you created an account with an Apple ID and password. You can use these to access iCloud and can skip ahead to the section, "Using Your iCloud Website."

▶ **Find My iPhone.** If you obtained a free Find My iPhone account, you can log in to iCloud using the same Apple ID and can jump ahead to the section, "Using Your iCloud Website."

▶ **MobileMe or .Mac.** If you've used either of these forerunners to iCloud, you are ready to start working with iCloud. If you're a current MobileMe user, go to the section, "Converting MobileMe to iCloud."

> NOTE: **Apple ID and iOS Devices**
>
> The first time you start up a new iOS device or one that has been restored as a new device, you're prompted to create an Apple ID or sign into an existing one. If you created an Apple ID or enabled iCloud at that time, you can skip to the section, "Using Your iCloud Website." If you didn't create an account at that time, continue to the next section.

If you don't have one of these accounts already, obtaining an iCloud account is pretty simple. You can get one on an iOS device, a Mac, or via iTunes on any kind of computer.

Creating an iCloud Account on an iOS Device

To create an iCloud account on an iOS device, perform the following steps:

1. Tap **Settings** on the Home screen. The Settings app opens.

2. Tap **iCloud**.

3. Tap **Get a Free Apple ID**. The New Account dialog appears, as shown in Figure 1.2.

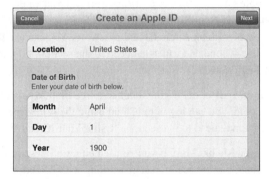

FIGURE 1.2   To create an Apple ID, simply fill out a series of forms.

4. Tap **Location**.

5. Tap your **location**.

6. Enter your date of birth by tapping **Month**, **Day**, and **Year** and use the selection tools or keyboard to enter the information.

7. Tap **Next**.

8. To use an email address that isn't already associated with an Apple ID, tap **Use an existing email address** or to create a new @me.com email address, tap **Get a free @me.com** email address.

9. If you chose to use an existing email address, enter it in the Email field; if you elected to create a new one, enter the address you want to use (everything before the @).

10. Enter your first and last name.

11. Create your password by entering it twice.

12. Tap **Question** and then tap the security question you want to use.

13. Enter the answer to your security question.

14. Tap **Next**. If the address you created is already in use, you see a warning message, and an alternate address is created for you. You can use that one or edit it and tap **Next** again. Repeat this process until your new address can be created.

15. Read the terms and conditions (yeah, right) and tap **Agree**.

16. Tap **Agree** again. Your Apple ID is created, and you are logged into iCloud. (If the account was created but you weren't able to log in for some reason, follow the instructions in Lessons 2, 3, and 4.)

If you used an existing email, a confirmation email is sent to that address. When you click the link in that email, your Apple ID and iCloud account become active. Skip to the section, "Using Your iCloud Website."

TIP: **Yet Another Way**

You can also use the My Apple ID website to create an Apple ID. As you learn later in this lesson, you can use this website to reset your password or find out what your Apple ID is as well.

Obtaining an iCloud Account on a Mac

You can create an iCloud account through the iCloud control pane of the
System Preferences application as follows:

1. Open the System Preferences application.

2. Click the **iCloud** icon. The iCloud pane opens.

3. Click **Create an Apple ID**.

4. Follow the onscreen instructions to complete the process.

When finished, you are logged into your new iCloud account and can skip
to the section, "Using Your iCloud Website."

Creating an iCloud Account via the iTunes Store

You can use an Apple ID to make purchases in the iTunes Store. You can
use iTunes to create an Apple ID for the store, which also creates your
iCloud account. Here's how:

NOTE: **Caveats**

If you want to create a new email address to use with iCloud, don't
use the iTunes method. Instead, create the account using an iOS
device or by using the appleid.apple.com website. Although using
iCloud is free, you have to provide payment information to create
an iTunes Store account. If you don't want to provide this, use one
of the other methods to create your account.

---

1. Open iTunes.

2. Click the **Sign In** link in the upper-right corner of the window.
   (If you see an account name here instead of the Sign In link, an
   account is already signed in. You can use that account for iCloud
   or click the account and sign out to see the Sign In link.)

3. In the resulting dialog box, click **Create New Account**, as shown
   in Figure 1.3. You see the Welcome to the iTunes Store screen.

FIGURE 1.3 You can create a new Apple ID via iTunes, which you can use for the iTunes Store and iCloud.

4. Click **Continue**.

5. Read the legalese, check the check box, and click **Agree**. You see the Provide Apple ID Details screen.

6. Enter the email address you want to use as your Apple ID.

7. Create your password.

8. Create your security question and answer.

9. Enter your data of birth.

10. Check the check boxes to receive emails or uncheck them if you don't want emails.

11. Click **Continue**, as shown in Figure 1.4.

12. Complete the Provide a Payment Method screen. Even though iCloud accounts are free, you need to enter payment information because that is required for an account on the iTunes Store.

13. Click **Create an Apple ID**. Your account is created.

14. When you receive the confirmation email, click the link it contains. Your Apple ID account is ready to use for iCloud.

After you confirm your account, skip to the section, "Using Your iCloud Website."

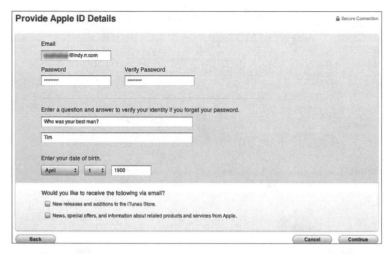

FIGURE 1.4   You can use an existing email address when you create an Apple ID via iTunes.

Converting MobileMe to iCloud

If you use or did use the MobileMe service, you are already set up to use iCloud. All you need to do is move your MobileMe account to iCloud by performing the following steps:

1. Use a web browser and go to me.com/move. (To see which web browsers you can use, see the section, "Using Your iCloud Website.")

2. Enter your MobileMe account information and click **Sign In**.

3. Click **Get Started**. You see that your calendars and contacts are moved from MobileMe to iCloud.

4. Click **Next**. You see that you can use the MobileMe Gallery, iDisk, and iWeb website until June 30, 2012.

5. Click **Next**. You see that some MobileMe features won't be available after you make the move.

6. Click **Next**. You see a list of hardware and software requirements for iCloud.

7. Check the **check box** to indicate that the devices you want to use meet the requirements.

8. Click **Next**. A warning that your contacts and bookmarks will be uploaded from your devices instead of from me.com appears. Be sure that at least one of your devices has your current contact information and bookmarks on it before you make the move.

9. Click **Next**. You see a reminder to back up your data before completing the move.

10. Click **Next**.

11. Check the **check box** to agree to the terms and conditions.

12. Click **Move to iCloud**, as shown in Figure 1.5. The move process takes place. When it is complete, you see a reminder to watch for prompts on your devices that are signed into MobileMe.

13. If you have any devices signed into your MobileMe account, look for alerts on those devices and follow the onscreen instructions to move from MobileMe to iCloud on each device.

14. In your web browser, click **Finished Setting Up**. You see the completion screen.

When you've moved your account to iCloud, you're ready for the next section.

Using Your iCloud Website

With your iCloud account, you get a useful website too. The website has applications you can use for your email, contacts, and calendars. You can also use the Find My iPhone feature to locate a device and to secure it if it is out of your control. And you can store and access documents there. All of these features are covered in later lessons.

FIGURE 1.5   This screen confirms you are now ready to move from MobileMe to iCloud.

In this section, you learn how to access your website, choose applications, and manage your iCloud account.

To use your iCloud website, you must use one of the following web browsers:

► Safari, version 5 or later

► Firefox, version 5 or later

► Internet Explorer, version 8 or later

► Chrome, version 12 or later

Logging Into Your Website

Logging into your iCloud website isn't challenging, as you can see:

1. Move to icloud.com.

2. Enter your iCloud **Apple ID**.

3. Enter your **Apple ID password**.

4. To save your information on the computer so you can move
    directly into your website when you come back to this address,
    check the **Keep me signed in** check box, as shown in Figure 1.6.

FIGURE 1.6   You can remain signed into your iCloud website to make it
even easier to access.

5. Click the **right-facing arrow** or press **Enter** or **Return**. You log
    into your website and work with your web applications or man-
    age your account.

Working with iCloud Web Applications

When you first log into your website, you see icons for each of the applications across the center of the window, as shown in Figure 1.7. The icons are
labeled, so it's easy to tell what they do even if you don't recognize them.

FIGURE 1.7   Click an application's icon to work with it.

In the upper-right corner of the window, you see your name, the Sign Out link, and the Help button.

If you click your **name**, you see the Account dialog box. Here, you can choose a photo to be associated with your account, choose the language you want to use, and set the time zone. If you click the **Advanced** link, you can reset your Photo Stream. When you're done making changes, click **Done**.

If you ever want to sign out of your website, such as if someone else is going to be using the computer, click the **Sign Out** link.

You can get iCloud help by clicking the **Help** button.

To use an application, simply click its icon, and you move into that application; Figure 1.8 shows the Contacts application as an example.

To change applications, click the **Cloud** button located in the upper-left corner of the current application's window. You move back to the screen shown in Figure 1.7 and can choose a different application by clicking its icon.

FIGURE 1.8   Here, you see the iCloud Contacts application.

NOTE: **Going Back Where You've Been**

Whenever you move back to your icloud.com website, you move back into the application you used most recently. Click the **Cloud** button to see the icons for and switch to any of the other applications.

Managing Your Account and Apple ID

To manage your account, if you ever forget your Apple ID or password, or if you want to reset your password, you can use the My Apple ID website.

To access it, use a web browser to move to appleid.apple.com. Here, you can do the following:

▶ To create a new Apple ID, click the **Create an Apple ID** button and follow the onscreen instructions.

▶ If you think you have an Apple ID but aren't sure, click the **Find Out** link and follow the onscreen instructions.

▶ To reset your password, click the **Reset your password** link and follow the onscreen instructions.

▶ To manage your account, click **Manage your account**. Sign into your account. Here, you can change various aspects of your account including your identification and email addresses, password and security information, addresses, phone numbers, and language and contact preferences. To edit an area, you click its link along the left side of the window; the tools you use to make changes appear in the right side of the window.

Summary

In this lesson, you learned about iCloud, how to obtain an iCloud account, and how to use your iCloud website. In the next lesson, you learn how to configure iCloud on an iOS device.

LESSON 2

Configuring iCloud on an iPhone, iPod touch, or iPad

In this lesson, you learn how to set up an iPhone, iPod touch, or iPad to use iCloud.

Configuring iCloud on an iOS Device

iCloud was designed for Apple's iOS devices: iPhone, iPod touch, and iPad. As you learned in Lesson 1, "Getting Started with Your iCloud Account and Website," when you configure an iCloud account on one of these devices, you get all kinds of benefits, such as syncing your information across multiple devices, online backup, and so on.

The iCloud software is built into the iOS software, so all you need to do is to configure your iOS device to access your iCloud account. The steps to do this are nearly identical on an iPhone, iPod touch, or iPad. Of course, the screens look slightly different on each device, but the steps to configure iCloud are exactly the same, so you can follow along no matter which device you are using.

In some cases, you see the name of a specific kind of device in a figure or command, such as Find My iPhone. Rather than repeat each option (Find My iPhone, Find My iPod, or Find My iPad), the text includes just one of the terms. If you are using a different device, you see that device's name instead.

Configuring an iOS device to use iCloud is a two-part process. The first part is to do the basic configuration of your iCloud account. The second part is to determine how and when iCloud information is updated on your device. These topics are covered in the following two sections.

You can also perform advanced configuration of your iCloud account. This is optional and is covered in the next to last section of this lesson.

Performing Basic iCloud Configuration on an iOS Device

To configure your iCloud account on an iOS device, perform the following steps:

1. On the Home screen, tap **Settings**. The Settings app opens.

2. Tap **iCloud**. You move to the iCloud Settings screen. You're then prompted to enter your iCloud account information, as shown in Figure 2.1.

3. Enter your **Apple ID**.

4. Enter your **Apple ID password**.

5. Tap **Sign In**, and your iCloud account is configured on your device.

6. If you're prompted about merging information already in your iCloud account, tap **Don't Merge** if you don't want the information already on your device to be moved into your iCloud account or tap **Merge** if you do.

NOTE: **Merging Information**

If you previously synced information under your iCloud account, such as calendars, when you enable syncing for that information, you are prompted to Merge or Don't Merge. If you tap Merge, the information you previously synced combines with the information already stored in your iCloud account. If you choose Don't Merge, you are prompted to Keep or Delete. If you tap Keep, the information you previously synced is kept on the device. If you tap Delete and then tap Delete again at the warning prompt, the information you previously synced is deleted from the device.

FIGURE 2.1   Enter your Apple ID and password and tap Sign In to access your iCloud account.

7. If prompted as shown in Figure 2.2, tap **Allow** to allow iCloud to access your device's location or **Don't Allow** if you don't want this to happen. You need to allow this for some features, such as Find My iPhone, to work. Next, you are prompted to choose the type of information you want to sync on your device.

8. Set the slider to the ON position next to each kind of information you want to sync on your device, as shown in Figure 2.3; for example, if Mail is set to ON, email syncs between your iCloud account and the device. If you set a slider to the OFF position, that type of information won't sync between your iCloud account and the device.

FIGURE 2.2   iCloud needs to be able to access your location for some features, such as Find My iPhone.

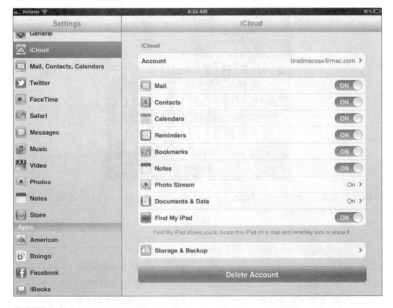

FIGURE 2.3   When a slider is set to ON, that type of information is included in the sync process.

Table 2.1 lists each of the options and provides a reference where you can find a detailed explanation of using each type of information in this book.

TABLE 2.1 iCloud Sync Options

Information	Description	Where to Find More Information
Mail	iCloud email	Lesson 9, "Configuring Your iCloud Email"
Contacts	Contact information	Lesson 10, "Using iCloud to Manage Your Contacts"
Calendars	Calendars	Lesson 11, "Using iCloud with Your Calendars"
Reminders	Reminders (tasks in Outlook)	Lesson 12, "Using iCloud to Sync Other Information"
Bookmarks	Safari or Internet Explorer bookmarks	Lesson 12, "Using iCloud to Sync Other Information"
Notes	Text notes	Lesson 12, "Using iCloud to Sync Other Information"
Photo Stream	Stores photos in the cloud	Lesson 7, "Using iCloud with Your Photos"
Documents & Data	Stores documents and other data in the cloud	Lesson 8, "Using iCloud with Your Documents"
Find My iPhone	Allows you to track your device's location	Lesson 13, "Using iCloud to Locate and Secure Your Devices"
Storage & Backup	Backs up the information on your device in the cloud and enables you to manage your online storage space	Lesson 14, "Using iCloud to Back Up and Restore Devices"

> **NOTE: The Missing Sliders**
>
> As you can see in Figure 2.3, Photo Stream and Documents & Data don't have sliders. When you tap those items, you move to screens that provide additional controls, which include the slider.

9. Tap **iCloud**. Your iCloud account configuration is complete. Next, determine how and when your iCloud information is updated on your device.

NOTE: **To Keep or Delete? That Is the Question**

If you move one of the sliders to the OFF position, you're prompted to keep the current data or delete it. For example, if you have previously used Calendar syncing, but then turn it OFF, you're prompted to keep or delete that information. If you keep the data, it remains on your device, but is not updated on the cloud. If you delete the data, it is removed from the device, but the information on the cloud remains.

NOTE: **To Merge or Not? That Is Also the Question**

If you re-enable information syncing that was previously not synced, you are prompted to merge or delete the information on your device. When you choose the merge option, the data on the device combines with that in the cloud. If you choose delete, the information on the device is replaced with that from the cloud.

Configuring Information Updates on an iOS Device

When you connect to the cloud via your iCloud account, information moves between the cloud and your devices. For example, you receive email messages in the cloud. When a device is configured to sync your email, new messages move from the server onto your device. Likewise, when you create email messages on your device, they move into the cloud.

There are three ways the information can move between your iOS devices and the cloud:

▶ **Push.** Push syncing occurs when the device is connected to the Internet and new information is on either the device or in the cloud. The new information is moved to or from the cloud as soon as it exists; this keeps information on the iOS device the most current because what you see on the device always reflects what is in the cloud. Push syncing has one definite drawback and another that is a matter of opinion. The definite drawback is that Push causes the largest energy use and shortest working time before you need to recharge your device, especially if the data in the cloud changes frequently. The drawback that is a matter of opinion is that some people (myself included) find Push intrusive and disruptive because notifications of new information can be almost constant and distracting from the task you are currently working on. It can certainly be annoying to others if you have audible notifications and are in meetings or other group situations. That said, some people prefer to have new information on their devices as soon as possible and are willing to accept shorter times between charges and more frequent interruptions.

▶ **Fetch.** Fetch syncing is automatic but is done according to a schedule, such as every 30 minutes. This provides automatic syncing but uses significantly less battery power than Push. And because notifications only occur when the scheduled sync happens, it can be less intrusive and distracting than Push syncing.

▶ **Manual.** Manual syncing occurs only when you start the process by moving into the related app. For example, when you open the Mail app, your device checks for new messages and downloads any that have been added to the cloud since the last time you checked. The downside of manual syncing is that you have to take action to sync your device. The upside is that you get information exactly when you want to deal with it. Unless you frequently sync manually, this option also uses the least battery power.

The option that is best for you depends on how much information you receive and whether or not you want to be immediately notified when you receive it. Because of improved battery life and automatic syncing, I recommend you start with the Fetch option. You can adjust the time intervals for syncing to ensure you get information to suit your preference while saving power compared to Push. You can always change or tweak the settings to suit your preferences over time.

To configure how syncing occurs, perform the following steps:

1. Tap **Settings** on the Home screen. The Settings app opens.

2. Tap **Mail, Contacts, Calendars**.

3. Tap **Fetch New Data**. You see the Fetch New Data screen as shown in Figure 2.4.

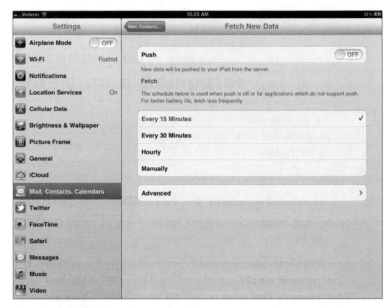

FIGURE 2.4   With these settings, this iPad syncs every 15 minutes.

4. If you want to use Push syncing, set the Push slider to the ON position. This setting impacts all your wirelessly synced accounts. If you want to disable Push for all accounts, set the slider to the OFF position. Even if you enable push, you need to configure the Fetch interval that will be used when Push isn't available.

5. In the Fetch section, tap the **amount of time** when you want to sync information when Push is OFF or is not available. The options are Every 15 Minutes, Every 30 Minutes, or Hourly.

6. If you want to use Manual syncing only, tap **Manually**. If Push is ON, it overrules this setting, so if you choose only Manual syncing, Push must be OFF, too. If Push is ON, the Manually option only applies when Push is not available. The iCloud account is ready to use and its information syncs according to your settings.

TIP: **Advanced Syncing**

You can have multiple accounts configured on your devices. In addition to your iCloud account, you might also have Gmail, Exchange, or other types of accounts. The settings on the Fetch New Data screen apply to all your accounts. Tap Advanced on this screen to see the Advanced screen. Here, you can configure the sync settings for each account individually by tapping the account. You move to that account's Select Schedule screen and then tap Push, Fetch, or Manual. (If an account doesn't support Push syncing, you won't see that option on its sync settings screen.) The setting on this screen applies only to that account. For example, you might want to have your work-related accounts sync automatically with Fetch and use Manual syncing for your personal accounts.

Performing Advanced iCloud Account Configurations

The information in this section is optional, and you can probably do most of what you want with iCloud without ever using it. However, it's good to be aware of these options in case you'd like to tweak your account further.

To access these advanced options, do the following:

1. On the Home screen, tap **Settings**. The Settings app opens.

2. Tap **iCloud**. You move to the iCloud settings screen.

3. Tap **Account** at the top of the screen. The Account window pops up, as shown in Figure 2.5.

FIGURE 2.5   You can use this window to perform advanced configuration of your iCloud account.

This window consists of three sections:

▶ **iCloud Account Information.** Here, you can change or re-enter your password and change the description of your account; the default name is iCloud, but you might want to change it to be your Apple ID or some other more personalized term.

▶ **Storage Plan.** This section provides your current iCloud storage; the default is 5GB. If you've upgraded your storage space, you see your current amount and what your annual fee is for this amount. If you tap the storage space icon, you can change the amount of space allowed under your account. If you tap **Payment Information**, you can change the payment details for your account. More information about managing the storage space for your iCloud account is provided in Lesson 1.

▶ **Advanced.** This option enables you to further configure your
  iCloud email. These options are explained in the following text.

If you tap **Mail** at the bottom of the screen, you can do even more configuration of your email account, as shown in Figure 2.6.

FIGURE 2.6   The Mail window provides additional configuration for your
iCloud email account.

The options you can configure on this window include

▶ **Name.** This is the name shown in the From field in emails you
  send. The default is the name associated with your iCloud
  account, but you can change it to something else.

▶ **SMTP.** This enables you to change the server through which
  your email is sent. (You should not have to ever change the
  server associated with your iCloud account.) You can also add
  more SMTP servers that can be used if the iCloud server is not
  available for some reason. To do this, tap **SMTP** on the Mail
  screen. Then tap **Add Server** and enter the server's address and

other information. When you send email from your iCloud account, the Mail app attempts to use the iCloud SMTP server first. If that fails, it will try the other servers on the list.

NOTE: **SMTP**

In case you are wondering, SMTP is the acronym for Simple Mail Transfer Protocol, which is the protocol iCloud uses to send email messages. If you weren't wondering, never mind.

▶ **Archive Messages.** If you set this slider to ON, messages you delete are saved in your iCloud's Archive folder instead of the Trash folder. This option is useful if you want to be able to delete email messages but always be able to go back to them in the future. However, messages stored in the Archive folder count against your iCloud storage space allocation. If you deal with a lot of messages and only have the default 5GB of storage space, your deleted messages can take up a significant amount of your space.

▶ **Advanced.** If you tap **Advanced** at the bottom of the Mail screen, you can set the behaviors of your mailboxes. These include where draft, sent, and deleted messages are stored, when deleted messages are removed from the server (the default is one week), and the S/MIME setting (see the following note).

You don't have to adjust any of these for your iCloud account to work fine for you, but if you are interested in tweaking the configuration further, check out these settings.

NOTE: **S/MIME**

Secure/Multipurpose Internet Mail Extensions (S/MIME) are a means to encrypt emails so that a key is required to be able to decrypt the information contained in them. To use S/MIME, you must install a certificate on your device for any account that uses these extensions. iCloud doesn't support this technology. If you do have access to an account that supports S/MIME, you need the certificate, key, and configuration information from the account provider to be able to configure it on your device.

Summary

In this lesson, you learned how to configure an iOS device to use iCloud. In the next lesson, you learn how to set up iCloud on a Macintosh computer.

LESSON 3

Configuring iCloud on Macintosh Computers

In this lesson, you learn how to configure your iCloud account on a Macintosh computer.

Logging Into Your iCloud Account

The iCloud software is built into Mac OS X. To start using it, you simply need to log into your iCloud account using the following steps:

> NOTE: **Mac OS X, v 10.7.2 or Later**
> To use iCloud's full functionality, your Mac must be running Mac OS X Lion, version 10.7.2 or later. If you are using an earlier version of Mac OS X Lion, you can upgrade by choosing Software Update on the Apple menu. If you aren't using Mac OS X Lion yet, you can purchase it using the App Store application.

1. Open the System Preferences application.

2. Click **iCloud**. The iCloud pane opens, as shown in Figure 3.1.

3. Enter your **Apple ID**.

4. Enter your **Apple ID password**.

5. Click **Sign In**. Your Mac logs into your iCloud account. You're prompted to use iCloud for specific syncing, as shown in Figure 3.2.

FIGURE 3.1   To start using iCloud on your Mac, log into your iCloud account.

FIGURE 3.2   These settings enable or disable information from iCloud syncing.

6. If you don't want to sync information, uncheck the **Use iCloud for contacts, calendars, and bookmarks** check box. You can reconfigure this later, so it doesn't really matter if you leave this enabled or not.

7. Uncheck the **Use Find My Mac** check box if you don't want to use this service that can locate your Mac. You can reconfigure this later, so it doesn't really matter if you leave this enabled or not.

8. Click **Next**.

9. If you enabled Find My Mac, click **Allow** to allow iCloud to use Location Services to locate your Mac. iCloud services begin working, and the information you enabled is synced with your iCloud account. Now you're ready to perform more detailed configurations of iCloud services.

Configuring and Managing Your iCloud Services

You can configure and manage the iCloud services you use by completing the following steps:

1. Open the System Preferences application.

2. Click **iCloud**. The iCloud pane opens, as shown in Figure 3.3. In the right part of the pane, you see the iCloud services available on your Mac. If a service's check box is checked, that information, such as Calendars, is being synced with the cloud, or the service, such as Back to My Mac, is enabled on your computer. At the bottom of the pane, you see the disk use gauge and Manage button that impacts your iCloud storage space (more on this shortly). In the left part of the pane, you see the Apple ID currently logged in and the buttons you can use to manage your iCloud account.

3. To enable specific information to be included in the sync process or to activate a service, check its check box; if you uncheck a check box, that information is removed from the sync process or the service is disabled. Table 3.1 lists the options and shows you where to get additional related information.

FIGURE 3.3   Use the iCloud pane to configure and manage iCloud services on your Mac.

TABLE 3.1   iCloud Options on a Mac

Information	Description	Where to Find More Information
Mail & Notes	iCloud email and notes	Lesson 9, "Configuring Your iCloud Email" (email)
		Lesson 12, "Using iCloud to Sync Other Information" (notes)
Contacts	Contact information	Lesson 10, "Using iCloud to Manage Your Contacts"
Calendars	Calendars	Lesson 11, "Using iCloud with Your Calendars"
Bookmarks	Safari bookmarks	Lesson 12, "Using iCloud to Sync Other Information"
Notes	Text notes	Lesson 12, "Using iCloud to Sync Other Information"
Photo Stream	Photo storage in the cloud	Lesson 7, "Using iCloud with Your Photos"
Documents & Data	Stores documents in the cloud	Lesson 8, "Using iCloud with Your Documents"

TABLE 3.1 iCloud Options on a Mac

Information	Description	Where to Find More Information
Back to My Mac	Enables you to control your Mac over the Internet	"Using the Back to My Mac Feature" later in this lesson
Find My Mac	Allows you to track your Mac's current location	Lesson 13, "Using iCloud to Locate and Secure Your Devices"

Here are some other pointers to keep in mind as you work with the iCloud pane of the System Preferences application:

▶ When you disable information syncing, you're prompted to either keep or delete the iCloud information that is currently stored on your Mac. If you select the **Keep** option, the sync process is stopped, but the information that has previously been synced is removed from your computer. If you select the **Delete** option, the information from iCloud is removed from your computer.

▶ The gauge at the bottom of the pane shows your current disk use. The more the bar is filled in, the more iCloud storage space you are currently using. If you click the **Manage** button, the Manage Storage sheet appears, as shown in Figure 3.4. In the left pane of the window, you see the services and applications that are currently using storage space and how much space each is using. When you select an application, you see the documents currently being stored for that application and how much space each document is consuming. Click **Done** to close the sheet.

TIP: **Freeing Space**
You can delete a document by selecting it and clicking **Delete**. You can delete all the documents for an application by selecting the application and clicking **Delete All**. Of course, you don't want to do either of these unless you are sure you don't need the documents any more or you have them stored in a different location.

FIGURE 3.4   Here, you see how your iCloud disk space is being used.

▶ If you click the **Account Details** button, a sheet showing your name and a description of your iCloud appears. You can change this information by editing it and clicking **OK**. This doesn't impact your account itself, but does change how information about the account appears, such as the name shown in the From field on emails you send.

▶ You can sign out of your iCloud account by clicking **Sign Out**. You're prompted to keep or delete the iCloud information currently on your Mac. When you make your choice, you are logged out of your iCloud account. The iCloud pane returns to the one that allows you to sign into your account. You can sign back into your account or sign into a different iCloud account.

NOTE: **One iCloud Account at a Time**

Although it's possible for you to have more than one iCloud account, you can only use one at a time for each user account on your Mac.

Using the Back to My Mac Feature

The Back to My Mac feature enables you to access your Mac over the Internet. To use Back to My Mac, the following conditions must be true:

▶ You must be logged into the same iCloud account on your current Mac and the one you are going to access via Back to My Mac.

▶ Back to My Mac must be enabled on the computer you are going to access and the one you are currently using.

▶ The computer you are accessing must be running, your user account must be active, and the computer can't be sleeping. (Ensure the **Wake for network access** check box on the Energy Saver pane is selected.)

When these conditions are met, you can access the computer by selecting it in the Sharing section of the Sidebar in a Finder window. You can click **Connect As** to log into that computer to access its files and folders or Share Screen to control the computer from your current computer.

Summary

In this lesson, you learned how to set up your iCloud account on a Macintosh computer. In the next lesson, you learn how to configure your iCloud account on a Windows PC.

LESSON 4

Configuring iCloud on Windows Computers

In this lesson, you learn how to configure your iCloud account on a Windows computer.

Downloading and Installing the iCloud Control Panel

To use iCloud with a Windows PC, you need to download and install the iCloud control panel. Here's how:

1. Open a web browser and go to http://support.apple.com/kb/DL1455.

2. Click **Download**.

3. At the prompt, click **Run**. The software is downloaded to your computer, and the installer runs.

4. Click **Run** at the prompt.

5. Follow the onscreen instructions to complete the installation of the iCloud control panel.

6. When the installation is complete, click **Finish**. You are ready to log into your iCloud account.

NOTE: **Requirements for iCloud**

To use iCloud on a Windows PC, you must be running Microsoft Windows Vista SP2 or Windows 7. To use your iCloud website and to sync bookmarks, you must use Safari 5.1.1 or Internet Explorer 8 or later. For calendar and contact syncing, Microsoft Outlook 2007 or 2010 are recommended.

Logging Into Your iCloud Account

To start using iCloud, you need to log into your iCloud account using the following steps:

1. Open the iCloud control panel, as shown in Figure 4.1.

FIGURE 4.1   To start using iCloud on your Windows PC, log into your iCloud account.

2. Enter your **Apple ID**.

3. Enter your **Apple ID password**.

4. Click **Sign In**. You log into your iCloud account, as shown in Figure 4.2. iCloud services become available, and you're ready to configure the specific services you want to use on the control panel, which now shows the services instead of the sign-in tools.

FIGURE 4.2   These settings enable or disable information syncing and services for your iCloud account.

Configuring and Managing Your iCloud Services

You can configure and manage the iCloud services you use by completing the following steps:

1. Open the iCloud control panel. As shown in Figure 4.3, in the right part of the pane, you see the iCloud services that are available on your Windows PC. If a service's check box is checked, that information, such as Calendars & Tasks with Outlook, is being synced with the cloud or the service, such as Photo Stream, is enabled on your computer. At the bottom of the pane, you see the disk use gauge and Manage button that impacts your iCloud storage space (more on this shortly). In the left part of the pane, you see the Apple ID currently logged in.

2. Check the **Show the iCloud status in System Tray** check box if you want to be able to access the iCloud control panel or get iCloud help by clicking the iCloud icon on the System Tray.

FIGURE 4.3   Use the iCloud pane to configure the services you use on your Windows PC.

3. To enable specific information to be included in the sync process or to activate a service, check its check box, as shown in Figure 4.3; if you uncheck a check box, that information is removed from the sync process or the service is disabled. Some choices have an Options button that you can click to make additional selections. Table 4.1 provides a list of the information or services you can select and shows you where to get more information about them.

TABLE 4.1   iCloud Options on a Windows PC

Information	Description	Where to Find More Information
Mail with Outlook	iCloud email	Lesson 9, "Configuring Your iCloud Email" (email)
Contacts with Outlook	Contact information	Lesson 10, "Using iCloud to Manage Your Contacts"
Calendars & Tasks with Outlook	Calendars iCloud reminders and Outlook tasks	Lesson 11, "Using iCloud with Your Calendars" (calendars) Lesson 12, "Using iCloud to Sync Other Information" (tasks/reminders)

TABLE 4.1   iCloud Options on a Windows PC

Information	Description	Where to Find More Information
Bookmarks with Internet Explorer or Bookmarks with Safari	Safari or Internet Explorer bookmarks	Lesson 12, "Using iCloud to Sync Other Information"
Photo Stream	Photo storage in the cloud	Lesson 7, "Using iCloud with Your Photos"

Here are some other pointers to keep in mind as you work with the iCloud control panel:

▶ When you disable information syncing, you're prompted to keep or delete the iCloud information that is currently stored on your computer. If you select the **Keep** option, the sync process is stopped, but the information that has previously been synced remains on your computer. If you select the **Delete** option, the information from iCloud is removed from your computer.

▶ The gauge at the bottom of the pane shows your current storage space use. The more the bar is filled in, the more iCloud storage space is currently being used. Click the **Manage** button, and the Manage Storage dialog box appears, as shown in Figure 4.4. In the left pane of the window, you see the services and applications that are currently using your storage space and how much space each is using. When you select an application, you see the documents currently being stored for that application and how much space each document is consuming. If you select a service, such as **Backups**, you see how that service is using your iCloud storage space. Click **Done** to close the sheet.

> TIP: **Freeing Space**
> You can delete a document by selecting it and clicking **Delete**. You can delete all the documents for an application by selecting the application and clicking **Delete All**. Of course, you don't want to do either of these unless you are sure you don't need the documents

any more or you have them stored in a different location. If you previously backed up a device to your iCloud account but no longer need to do this, select **Backups**, click the **device**, and click **Delete**.

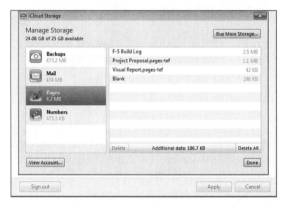

FIGURE 4.4   Here, you see how your iCloud disk space is being used.

▶ On the iCloud Storage dialog box, click **View Account**, enter your account's password, and click **View Account** again. The storage information is replaced by the Apple ID Summary dialog box. Here, you can change the storage plan for your account (click the upper **Change** button), edit your payment information (click the **Edit** button), or change the country or region associated with your account (click the lower **Change** button).

▶ Click the **Buy More Storage** button on the iCloud Storage dialog box, and you see the Buy More Storage dialog box, as shown in Figure 4.5. The highlighted amount with the check mark is your current plan. To upgrade the space available to you, click the option you want to select, click **Next**, and then follow the onscreen instructions to add more space to your account. If you upgraded your storage and decide you want to reduce it again, click the **Downgrade Options** button and follow the onscreen instructions to reduce the space allocated to your account.

FIGURE 4.5 Use this dialog to view your current storage plan or to upgrade the amount of space available.

► You can sign out of your iCloud account by clicking **Sign Out** on the iCloud control panel. You're prompted to keep or delete the iCloud information currently on your computer. After you make a choice, you are logged out of your iCloud account. The iCloud control panel returns to the state that allows you to sign into your account. You can sign back into your account or sign into a different iCloud account.

> NOTE: **One iCloud Account at a Time**
> Although it's possible for you to have more than one iCloud account, you can only access one at a time for each user account on your computer.

Summary

In this lesson, you learned how to set up your iCloud account on a Windows computer. In the next lesson, you learn how to use iCloud for music, apps, and books.

LESSON 5

Using iCloud with Your iTunes Music, Apps, and Books

In this lesson, you learn how to use iCloud to make sure music, apps, and books you purchase from the iTunes Store are always available to you on any device.

Understanding Automatic iTunes Store Purchase Downloading

The iTunes Store offers lots of great audio, video, and book content that you can purchase, download, and enjoy on iOS devices and computers. Before iCloud, to get the same content on more than one device, you had to use the sync process to move the content into iTunes on a computer (unless it was purchased on the computer of course) and then use iTunes to sync the content onto other devices. And it was even more work to make the content available on both a Mac and a PC.

iCloud takes away these hassles in a couple of ways. First, you can configure all your equipment (computers and iOS devices) to automatically download any future music, app, or book purchases you make from the iTunes Store. Second, you can easily download any past purchases of music, TV shows, apps, or books directly onto your iOS devices.

Configuring your devices for automatic downloading is covered in a section for each type of device: iOS, Macs, and Windows PCs. You need to read only the sections that are relevant to the devices you use.

NOTE: **No Movies (or Podcasts) for You!**

You can't use iCloud to move movies you obtain from the iTunes Store onto your devices.

To get movies on your devices, you have to use the old-fashioned approach by moving the movies into your iTunes Library through the sync process (if they weren't purchased on the computer) and then using the sync process to move those movies onto your iOS devices.

Movies you rent can only exist on one device at a time. If you didn't rent the movie on the device on which you want to watch it, you need to move it back to your iTunes Library and from there move it onto a different device through the sync process.

The same is true of podcasts. To get them on all your devices, subscribe to them in iTunes on a computer and use the sync process to move them onto your iOS devices or download them directly onto each iOS device using the iTunes app.

Using iCloud to Download iTunes Store Purchases on an iOS Device

An iCloud account helps you get content you purchased from the iTunes Store onto your iOS device with ease; this works for music, TV shows, apps, and books. In this section, you learn two ways to use iCloud to get purchased content on your iOS device:

▶ Add newly purchased content automatically.

▶ Download previously purchased content.

NOTE: **A Third Way**

You can also use iTunes Match to stream music in your iTunes Library on an iOS device. This is explained in Lesson 6, "Using iTunes Match with Your Music."

Configuring Automatic Downloading of iTunes Store Purchases on an iOS Device

To configure automatic downloads to your iOS devices of the content you purchase from the iTunes Store, perform the following steps:

1. Tap **Settings**. The Settings app opens.

2. Tap **Store**. You move to the Store settings screen.

3. Set the status bar to the ON position for the types of content that you want downloaded to your device automatically, as shown in Figure 5.1.

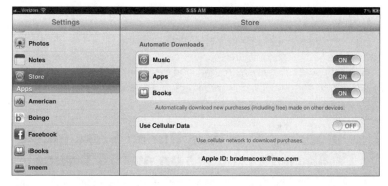

FIGURE 5.1   With this configuration, any music, apps, or books purchased from the iTunes Store on any iCloud-enabled device are automatically down-loaded to this iPad.

4. If you are configuring a device that supports a cellular data con-nection (iPhone or iPad) and you don't have an unlimited data plan, ensure that Use Cellular Data is OFF. If this is ON, content will be downloaded to your device when you use a cell network for data. This can consume significant amounts of data; if you have a limited data plan this can get expensive, so you should set this to OFF so content is only downloaded when you are on a Wi-Fi network.

TIP: **Apple ID**

At the bottom of the Store screen, you see the Apple ID currently logged in. If you tap this, you see a menu with a number of useful commands. You can use this menu to view your Apple ID, sign out of your account, or reset your password. If you sign out of your account, the Store screen only has the Sign In button. Tap this and sign into the Apple ID you want to use.

After you've done these steps, any content you enabled in step 3 is downloaded to the iOS device automatically when you purchase it from the iTunes Store. (This only affects future purchases, but in the next section, you learn how to get previously purchased content.)

TIP: **Downloading TV Show Purchases**

Although you can't configure your device to automatically download TV purchases, you can easily download any TV show purchases you've made in the past—as you learn in the next section.

Downloading Previous iTunes Store Music or TV Show Purchases on an iOS Device

You can download music or TV shows you've previously purchased to an iOS device using the iTunes app:

1. Open the iTunes app.

2. Tap **Purchased**.

3. If you are using an iPhone or iPod touch, tap **Music or TV Shows**, as shown in Figure 5.2; if you are using an iPad, tap the **View** button in the upper-left corner of the screen and then tap **Music** or **TV Shows**. The rest of these steps show downloading music by selecting the Music option, but the steps to download TV shows are similar.

NOTE: **Free Is Purchased**

In the context of iTunes Store content, free stuff is treated like content you have to pay for. So you use the same tools to download content whether it is free or has a purchase price.

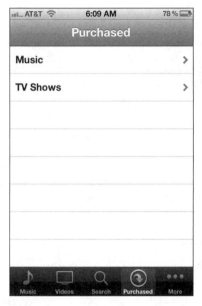

FIGURE 5.2   The Purchased screen in the iTunes app enables you to download music or TV shows.

  4. Tap **Not On This** *Device* tab, where *Device* is the type of device you are using, such as an iPhone or iPad. The list shows all the music you've purchased from the iTunes Store but that is not currently stored on the device. If you are using an iPad, you see an index of all your purchased content that is not on the iPad along the left side of the screen. If you are using an iPhone, the index fills the screen. At the top of the index, you see the number of songs that you've purchased that aren't on the device and the number of recent purchases. You can tap either of these to browse those lists of content. Below this, you see all the artists associated with content you haven't downloaded to the device; this works just like the lists in the Music app. You also see the number of tracks for each artist.

TIP: **Searching for Content in All the Right Places**

You can search for the purchased content you want to download by tapping the Search field, typing your search criteria, and tapping Search. The list of content is narrowed to only the items that match your search criteria. This can be a faster way to get to specific content you want to download.

NOTE: **iCloud Is Optional**

You don't have to be logged into your iCloud account to download previous TV show and music purchases. That feature is available to you based on your iTunes Store account.

---

5. Browse the list.

6. Tap the **artist** whose music you want to download. You see a list of content for that artist, organized into categories. On an iPad, you can choose which category you want to see, either albums or songs; if on an iPhone or iPod touch, you see the content organized by category.

7. On an iPad, tap **Songs** to see the content by song, as shown in Figure 5.3, or tap **Albums** to see it grouped by album instead. On an iPhone or iPod touch, you can browse the list of albums or tap **All Songs** to see the content by song, as shown in Figure 5.4.

TIP: **Sorting It All Out**

When you are viewing the content by Songs on an iPad, you can tap the Sort By button in the upper-right corner of the screen and choose Most Recent, Song Name, or Album to change how the content shown is sorted. If you are viewing the content by album, you can choose Most Recent or Album to sort by those attributes.

FIGURE 5.3   On an iPad, you can browse purchased music by song or by album; Songs is selected here.

FIGURE 5.4　On an iPhone or iPod touch, you see the content listed by album, or you can tap All Songs to see it by song instead.

8. Tap the **Download** button (the cloud icon with the downward pointing arrow) for the content you want to download. To download all the content, tap the **Download** button shown above all the content (iPad) or tap **Download All** (iPhone/iPod touch).

9. If prompted, enter your Apple ID password and tap **OK**. The content is downloaded to your device.

10. On an iPhone or iPod touch, tap **More** and then tap **Downloads**. Or on an iPad, tap the **Downloads** tab at the bottom of the screen to move to the Downloads screen so you can monitor the progress of the downloads. as shown in Figure 5.5. When all the content has been downloaded, the screen empties.

> TIP: **Not So Fast**
>
> To halt the download process, tap the **Pause** button next to content being downloaded. To start the download again, tap the **Resume** button (downward facing arrow).

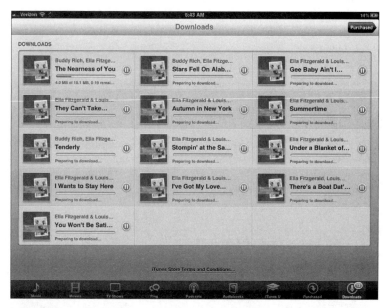

FIGURE 5.5   On the Downloads screen, you can monitor the progress of content being downloaded to your device.

Downloading Previous iTunes Book Purchases on an iOS Device

You can download books you've previously purchased to an iOS device using the iBooks app:

1. Open the iBooks app.

2. Tap the **Store** button.

3. Tap **Purchased**.

4. Tap **All** to see all your purchased books or tap **Not On This Device**, where *Device* is the name of the device you are using, to see books that haven't been downloaded yet.

5. To download a book, tap its **Download** button.

6. If prompted, enter your Apple ID password and tap **OK**. The book is downloaded to your device and becomes available in the Library.

NOTE: **Downloaded Before?**

If a book was previously downloaded to the device but was removed through the sync process, it won't appear on the Not On This *Device* tab. To download it again, tap the All tab. Books that have been previously downloaded to the device but are not currently stored on it have the Download button. Tap this to download the book to the device again.

NOTE: **iCloud Is Optional Here, Too**

Like music and TV shows, you can download books and apps you've purchased previously without being logged into your iCloud account because they are associated with your iTunes Store account.

Downloading Previous iTunes App Purchases on an iOS Device

You can download apps you've previously purchased to an iOS device using the App Store app:

1. Open the App Store app.

2. On an iPad, tap the **Purchased** tab; on an iPhone or iPod touch, tap the **Updates** tab and then tap **Purchased**. You see the Purchased Apps screen.

3. Tap **Not On This *Device***, where *Device* is the device you are using, to see apps you've purchased but not downloaded to the device. Figure 5.6 shows this screen on an iPad.

4. If you are using an iPad, tap **iPad** to see only apps specifically for an iPad or tap **iPhone** to see apps designed for iPhones/iPod touches.

FIGURE 5.6   The Not On This iPad tab shows apps that have not been downloaded to this device.

5. Tap the **Download** button for the app you want to add to the device.

NOTE: **Password or Not?**

If you've entered your Apple ID recently, such as if you have just downloaded something, you won't have to enter again for a while. When the password isn't required, the content downloads to your device without your password.

---

6. If prompted, enter your Apple ID password and tap **OK**. The Download button is replaced by a status button that shows the app being installed on your device. When the installation process is complete, you can use the app.

NOTE: **Syncing and Purchased Content**

When you sync your iOS devices to iTunes, any purchased content is copied into your iTunes Library automatically.

Using iCloud to Automatically Download iTunes Store Purchases on a Mac

You can configure iTunes on a Mac to automatically download your music, app, and book purchases so they are stored in your iTunes Library. This is useful to store your content, and you can use iTunes to enjoy the content on your Mac. Here's how to make this happen:

1. In iTunes, choose **iTunes**, **Preferences**.

2. Click the **Store** tab.

3. Check the **Music**, **Apps**, and **Books** check boxes if you want these types of content downloaded to your Mac automatically, as shown in Figure 5.7; if you leave a check box unchecked, that type of content won't be downloaded automatically.

4. Click **OK**. Any music, apps, or books you download from the iTunes Store are downloaded to your Mac automatically. no matter which device you use to download them.

TIP: **Home Sharing**

Though not part of iCloud, it can be useful to stream content in your computer's iTunes Library to other computers, iOS devices, or Apple TVs through the Home Sharing feature in iTunes. Turn on **Home Sharing** through the Advanced menu in iTunes and sign into the account associated with the content you want to share.

To access shared content on an iOS device, open the Music app, tap **More**, tap **Shared**, and tap the **name of the Library** on which you enabled Home Sharing. You can browse and play the content in that library.

On an Apple TV, choose **Computers**, choose **Turn On Home Sharing**, and then enter the **user name** and **password** for the Home Share account. You can then watch or listen to content in the Home Share library.

On a computer, open iTunes and click **Home Sharing** in the SHARED section of the Source list. Enter the sharing **Apple ID and password** and click **Create Home Share**. When you are logged in, you can select the **shared Library** to enjoy its content.

FIGURE 5.7 With these selections, music, apps, and books purchased on any device are automatically downloaded to this Mac.

Using iCloud to Automatically Download iTunes Store Purchases on a Windows PC

You can configure iTunes on a Windows PC to automatically download your music, app, and book purchases so they are stored in your iTunes Library. This is useful to store your content, and you can use iTunes to enjoy the content on your computer. To enable automatic downloads, perform the following steps:

1. In iTunes, choose **Edit**, **Preferences**.

2. Click the **Store** tab.

3. Check the **Music**, **Apps**, and **Books** check boxes if you want these types of content downloaded to your computer automatically, as shown in Figure 5.8; if you leave a check box unchecked, that type of content won't be downloaded automatically.

FIGURE 5.8   With these selections, music, apps, and books purchased on any device are downloaded automatically to this computer.

4. Click **OK**. Any music, apps, or books you download from the iTunes Store are downloaded to your Windows PC automatically, no matter which device you use to download them.

TIP: **Yet Another Way to Share**

You can share content in your iTunes Library with other computers on the same local network. Open iTunes Preferences. Click the **Sharing** tab. Click the **top** check box to share your library and then choose to share the entire library or only selected playlists. You can also configure a password if you want.

You can access libraries being shared by clicking on them in the SHARED section of the iTunes Source list. If required, enter the **password**. You can then select the **shared source** and browse and play its content.

Summary

In this lesson, you learned how to use iCloud so that you have all your music, app, and book purchases available on all your devices. In the next lesson, you learn how to use iTunes Match to stream your music to your iOS devices.

LESSON 6

Using iTunes Match with Your Music

In this lesson, you learn how to use iTunes Match to make your music available from the cloud so you can stream it to your iOS devices and computers.

Understanding iTunes Match

iTunes Match puts all of the music in your iTunes Library on the cloud so you can download and stream that music to your devices over the Internet. This makes your music available to you wherever you are (assuming you have an Internet connection in that location, of course). iTunes Match works for all the music in your Library, not just for music you've purchased from the iTunes Store (which, as you learned in Lesson 5, "Using iCloud with Your iTunes Music, Apps, and Books," you can download directly to any of your devices at any time). For example, if you've imported music from a CD into your Library instead of buying that music in the iTunes Store, you can download it to your device just as easily as if you had purchased it in the iTunes Store. This eliminates the need to sync your music on your devices because you always have the music you want to hear at any point in time; you always see all the music in your iTunes Library on all the devices that are configured to use iTunes Match. If music you want to hear isn't currently stored on your device, you just tap the **Download** button and when the music starts to download, it also starts to play.

NOTE: **Match Account Not Computer**

It helps to realize the iTunes Match is tied to your Apple ID, not to a specific iTunes Library. If you enable iTunes Match on more than one computer, all the music from each computer is uploaded to the cloud, and each can download and play music from the cloud.

There are a couple of points about this service that you need to be aware of. First, if you want to use iTunes Match, you must pay for the service; the cost is currently $24.99 per year in the United States (it may have a different price in other areas). The second point is trivial, but worth noting—if you configure an iOS device to use iTunes Match, the Music tab of the Sync screen contains only a check box to indicate if you want your voice memos synced. All your music is always available to you on your device so there is no need to sync it.

NOTE: **Quality Counts**

iTunes Match music is delivered in the Advanced Audio Coding (AAC) format encoded at 256 kbps. If music in your iTunes Library is not already in this format, a temporary version in this format is created and then uploaded to the cloud. This format may actually be higher quality than the music that is permanently stored in your iTunes Library.

Whether or not you benefit from iTunes Match depends on your specific circumstances. If you only have music from the iTunes Store in your iTunes Library, you don't need iTunes Match because you can download any purchased music to your device at any time already for no additional cost. If your devices have enough space to store all the music in your iTunes Library along with all the other content you want on the device, you don't really need iTunes Match because you can store all your music on the device anyway. If you have a lot of music from sources other than the iTunes Store in your Library and your iOS device doesn't have enough space to store it all, iTunes Match may be right for you.

There are two basic steps to enabling iTunes Match. Step one is to activate iTunes Match in iTunes on a computer; this puts all your music in the cloud. Step two is to configure your devices to use iTunes Match.

After these two steps are done, you can listen to any of your music on your devices at any time.

> NOTE: **iTunes Match Caveats**
>
> iTunes Match uploads up to 25,000 songs, not counting those you have purchased from the iTunes Store. Song files over 200MB won't be uploaded to the cloud. Songs protected with Digital Rights Management (DRM) won't be uploaded unless your computer is authorized to play those songs.

Configuring and Managing iTunes Match in iTunes

To get started with iTunes Match, set it up in iTunes. This puts all your music on the cloud.

After you've configured iTunes to use iTunes Match, you can use its tools to manage your iTunes Match service.

Setting Up iTunes Match in iTunes

To start using iTunes Match, perform the following steps:

1. In iTunes, choose **Store**, **Turn On iTunes Match**. You move to the iTunes Match screen.

2. Click **Subscribe for $24.99 Per Year**.

3. Enter your **Apple ID password**.

4. Click **Subscribe**.

5. Follow the onscreen instructions to review or update your payment or other information as required. iTunes Match starts the upload process, which has three steps. During step 1, iTunes collects information about your iTunes Library. During step 2,

iTunes matches songs in your Library with those available in the iTunes Store, as shown in Figure 6.1; these songs immediately become available to play on your devices.

FIGURE 6.1   iTunes is matching music stored in the iTunes Library with songs available in the iTunes Store.

During step 3, iTunes uploads songs in your Library that aren't in the iTunes Store; this part of the process can take a while depending on the number of songs involved. You can use iTunes for other things during this process. You can check the progress at any time by selecting iTunes Match on the Source list. When the process is complete, you see how many songs are available to you in the cloud, as shown in Figure 6.2.

NOTE: **More on Music Uploading**

All the music in your iTunes Library falls into one of two situations. One is that the music is available in the iTunes Store; any music that falls into this category is immediately available on the cloud whether you purchased it in the iTunes Store or not. The other is that the music is not available in the iTunes Store; in this situation, the music is uploaded to the cloud.

6. Click **Done**. Your music is in the cloud and ready for you to listen to it from any of your devices.

FIGURE 6.2 This screen shows you that the match process is complete and how many songs are available to you on the cloud.

Managing iTunes Match in iTunes

Following are some tips to help you manage iTunes Match:

▶ If you add new music to your Library, such as importing a CD, you can refresh your music on the cloud by choosing **Store, Update iTunes Match**. iTunes Match goes through the three-step process again, which adds any new music in your iTunes Library to the cloud.

▶ When iTunes Match is active, the Music source in iTunes is marked with the cloud icon. When you select the **Music** source, you see a browser column with the cloud icon at the top, which indicates the iTunes Match status of the song. When you don't see any icon in this column, it means the song is available on the cloud. A cloud with a slash through indicates the song isn't eligible for iTunes Match for some reason; for example, digital booklets that you get with some music can't be added to the cloud. A cloud with an exclamation point means there was an error uploading the song; use the Update iTunes Match command to try to fix the problem. Two clouds with a slash through them indicates a duplicate; duplicates are not uploaded to the cloud. A cloud icon indicates the song has been matched but not yet uploaded.

▶ If you want to stop using iTunes Match, choose **Store, Turn Off iTunes Match**. Your music remains on the cloud, but the music in the iTunes Library is no longer matched.

▶ To re-enable iTunes Match, choose Store, Turn On iTunes Match. You move back to the iTunes Match screen. Click **Add This Computer**. iTunes Match goes through the three-step process of matching music again.

Listening to Your iTunes Match Music on an iOS Device

Before you can use iTunes Match on an iOS device, you need to configure the device to use iTunes Match as its source of music; you only have to do this once. After that is done, you can easily listen to any of your music on the iOS device.

Configuring an iOS Device to Use iTunes Match

Set up an iOS device to use iTunes Match by completing the following steps:

1. Tap **Settings**. The Settings app opens.

2. Tap **Music**.

3. Set the **iTunes Match** switch to ON.

4. Tap **Enable** at the prompt explaining that the music content on the device will be replaced.

5. If you want all the music available to you to be shown in the device, set **Show All Music** to ON, as shown in Figure 6.3; if you set this to OFF, only music that has been downloaded to the device is shown. The music content of your device becomes available via iTunes Match.

FIGURE 6.3   This iPhone is configured to get music from the cloud.

Listening to iTunes Match Music on an iOS Device

iTunes Match is nice because you don't have to worry about syncing the music in your iTunes Library to your device; any music in your iTunes Library is available for your listening pleasure. If the music you want to hear isn't already stored on the device, when you select it, it gets downloaded and begins to play.

Listening to music with iTunes Match is very similar to listening to music that you've moved onto your device via the sync process. The difference is that you may have to download the music to your device before it starts to play.

Music that needs to be downloaded to your device is marked with the cloud icon; if you don't see this icon, the music has already been downloaded, and you can listen to it immediately.

CAUTION: **Downloading Music via a Cellular Connection**

Music files are fairly large. If you have a device that uses a cellular data connection and there is a limit to how much data is included with your plan, you need to be careful with iTunes Match because you may exceed your data plan's limits, which can be quite expensive. To prevent iTunes Match music from being downloaded when you are using your cellular connection, move to the Settings app and tap **Store**. On the Store screen, set **Use Cellular Data** to OFF. In this state, you need to be connected to a Wi-Fi network to be able to download and stream music to the device. This is less convenient, but you won't risk overcharges from downloading too much data.

When iTunes Match is set up on your iOS device, finding and playing music is pretty similar to when your music is stored on the device. Use the Music app to browse or search for music to which you want to listen. All of your music is in one of the two following states:

▶ If the music doesn't have the cloud icon, it is already on your device and you can use the app's tools to play it.

▶ If the music is marked with the cloud icon, as shown in Figure 6.4, tap the **song** to start the download process and play the music. When enough of the music has been downloaded so that it can play smoothly, it starts to play.

FIGURE 6.4   Two songs of this album are downloaded; one is currently play-ing (marked with the speaker icon). Songs followed by the cloud icon are available to download and play.

Here are some additional points to ponder when it comes to using iTunes Match on an iOS device:

▶ If you have a slow connection, it might take a moment for a song that is downloading to start playing after you tap it.

▶ If you just want to download a song and listen to it later, tap the **cloud icon** instead of the song. The download status wheel replaces the icon and shows the progress of the download. When the song has been downloaded, the icon disappears, and the song is stored on your device.

▶ You can download entire albums, playlists, and other content by tapping the **Download All** button, which is located at the bottom of browsing screens.

▶ Tap **Shuffle** at the top of your screens to have the Music app randomly download and play content from the source you're browsing.

▶ If content is grayed out and doesn't have the cloud icon next to it, it is not available in the cloud so you can't download and play it. This is likely because it just hasn't been uploaded by iTunes Match yet. If you come back to the content at a later time, it will probably be available.

Listening to Your iTunes Match Music on a Computer

You can also use iTunes Match to listen to music on a computer. Similar to an iOS device, there are two steps to the process. First, add the computer to iTunes Match (you have to do this only once for the same Apple ID). Second, download and listen to music from the cloud.

Adding a Computer to iTunes Match

To be able to access your cloud music from a computer, perform the following steps:

1. In iTunes, log into the iTunes Store using the Apple ID for which you enabled iTunes Match by selecting **iTunes Store** on the Source list; if the Apple ID you are using isn't shown in the upper right corner, click the account shown or click **Sign In** and sign into your **Apple ID**.

2. Choose **Store, Turn On iTunes Match**.

3. Click **Add This Computer**.

4. Enter your account's password.

5. Click **Add This Computer**. iTunes starts the three-step iTunes Match process. Any music that is in the current computer's iTunes Library but isn't in the cloud is added to your music collection on the cloud. If this computer doesn't have much music stored on it, the process is completed fairly quickly.

6. When the process is completed, click **Done**, as shown in Figure 6.5. You're ready to listen to music from the cloud.

FIGURE 6.5   This Windows PC is connected to the cloud.

TIP: Add Music Anywhere

If you have iTunes Match enabled on all your computers and automatic downloads enabled on all your computers and iOS devices, where you purchase or upload music is irrelevant because it is available automatically on all your devices. Whenever you import a CD into iTunes, use the Store, Update iTunes Match to add that music to the cloud.

Listening to iTunes Match Music on a Computer

Listening to music from the cloud on a computer is a snap. When it is connected to iTunes Match, the Music source is marked with the cloud icon, as shown in Figure 6.6.

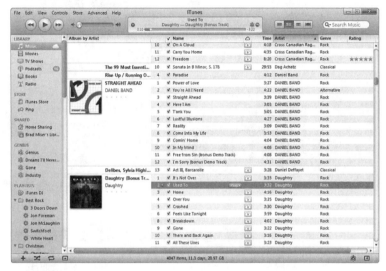

FIGURE 6.6   Songs without the cloud icon have been downloaded to the computer and are ready to play. Other songs are easy to download and play as well.

In iTunes, browse music as you normally would. Do any of the following to listen to music:

▶ If songs aren't marked with an icon, they are stored on the computer already and are ready to play whether the computer is connected to the Internet or not.

▶ To play a song without downloading it, select and play the song as you normally would. The song plays via streaming from the

Internet, but is not stored on the computer. The next time you play it, it plays via streaming again. The computer has to be connected to the Internet to stream music.

▶ To download a song, click its **cloud icon**. The song is downloaded to the computer and stored in the iTunes Library. You can play it without being connected to the Internet.

Summary

In this lesson, you learned how to use iTunes Match to access the music in your iTunes Library on any iOS device or computer. In the next lesson, you learn how to use iCloud's Photo Stream.

LESSON 7

Using iCloud with Your Photos

In this lesson, you learn how to take advantage of iCloud's Photo Stream to automatically have all of your photos on multiple devices.

Understanding Photo Stream

If you have more than one device with which you take, store, edit, or view photos, you'll probably find that Photo Stream is one of iCloud's most useful features. Photo Stream stores your photos in the cloud so that you can access them on any device. The great news is that this happens automatically; you don't have to worry about syncing your photos among your devices because Photo Stream handles this for you.

Each of your devices can add photos to your Photo Stream (sender) and download photos from the Photo Stream (receiver). (Note that an Apple TV can only receive photos from Photo Stream.) For example, you can take photos with your iPhone; the photos you take are automatically uploaded to your cloud. Those photos are then automatically downloaded, via Photo Stream, to all your devices on which Photo Stream is enabled (see Figure 7.1). You don't have to sync any of the devices to work with your photos; Photo Stream brings photos to and receives photos from each device automatically.

To use Photo Stream, you first configure it on each device. Once configured, how you work with your Photo Stream depends on the specific device. Throughout this lesson, there are sections devoted to working with Photo Stream on each type of device, and you just need to read the section that covers your specific devices.

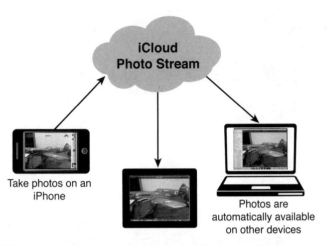

FIGURE 7.1   Photo Stream eliminates the need to manually sync photos on your devices.

The following are general points that will help you understand and use Photo Stream more effectively:

▶ When you take photos on an iOS device, they are uploaded to Photo Stream when you exit the Photos app and are connected to a Wi-Fi network (Photo Stream doesn't move photos over a cellular data connection). If you take photos while a device is not connected to a Wi-Fi network, they are uploaded the next time you connect it to a network.

▶ Photos are stored in your Photo Stream for 30 days.

▶ Because Photo Stream is not a long-term storage location, you need to make sure any photos you want to keep are stored in a permanent location.

▶ If you use Photo Stream with a Mac or a Windows PC, photos are permanently stored for you automatically. When a photo is added to your Photo Stream, it is downloaded onto your Mac (and stored in iPhoto '11 or Aperture 3.2) or Windows PC (and stored in the designated location) automatically. So, as long as you have a Mac or Windows PC set up to use Photo Stream, you don't have to worry about losing any of your photos.

▶ When you add photos to iPhoto or Aperture on a Mac or in the designated locations on a Windows PC, they are uploaded to your Photo Stream, too.

▶ On an iOS device, the Photo Stream album contains up to 1,000 photos. When you exceed that number, photos are removed from the Photo Stream album automatically. If you don't also use Photo Stream with a Mac or a Windows PC, you need to move the photos you want to keep from the Photo Stream album onto a permanent album on the iOS device (this is explained later in this lesson).

▶ An Apple TV can only download photos from the Photo Stream.

▶ Photos are stored in your Photo Stream at their full resolution. They download to a Mac or Windows PC at the full resolution as well. When they are downloaded to an iOS device or an Apple TV, the resolution is optimized for the device.

▶ Photo Stream supports the most common photographic formats, such as JPEG, TIFF, PNG, and RAW. Photo formats only become a potential concern when you add photos to a Mac or Windows PC that weren't taken with an iOS device or a digital camera, such as images you download from the Internet. These images have to be in a supported format to be uploaded to your Photo Stream.

▶ Photo Stream doesn't support video. If you take videos with an iOS device, they only become available on other devices when you sync the device to a computer and then move the video onto other devices through the sync process.

SIDEBAR: **Photo Stream and iCloud Space**

In case you are wondering, photos in your Photo Stream don't count against your iCloud storage space limit.

Using Photo Stream with iOS Devices

You could say that Photo Stream was designed with iOS devices in mind, and you'd be correct if you did. Photo Stream is an ideal way to make photos you take with one of these devices available on your other devices; it's also great because you can view and work with any of your photos on your iOS device as well.

> NOTE: **iOS 5 Required**
>
> To use Photo Stream, an iOS device must be running version 5 or later.

To use Photo Stream, enable it on each of your iOS devices. Then you can access your Photo Stream via the Photos app.

After Photo Stream is enabled, you don't need to do anything to upload photos you take with the device's camera to your cloud. This process happens automatically any time your device is connected to the Internet using a Wi-Fi network.

> NOTE: **Connect to Stream**
>
> An iPhone or iPad (with optional cellular capability) can use its cellular network or a Wi-Fi network while an iPod touch uses a Wi-Fi network to connect to the Internet. However, Photo Stream only works over a Wi-Fi connection. Any photos you take on a device while it isn't connected via Wi-Fi will be uploaded to the cloud as soon you connect to a Wi-Fi network. When you connect to a Wi-Fi network, any photos uploaded to the cloud since the device was last connected via Wi-Fi are downloaded to the device.

You can view and work with photos stored in your Photo Stream with the Photos app. This app enables you to view your Photo Stream photos, email them, tweet them, and so on. If you want to permanently store a photo contained in your Photo Stream on the iOS device, you can do that, too.

Enabling Photo Stream on an iOS Device

To start using Photo Stream on an iOS device, enable it with the following steps:

1. Open the Settings app.

2. Tap **iCloud**.

3. Tap **Photo Stream**.

4. Slide the Photo Stream switch to the ON position (see Figure 7.2). Your iOS device immediately downloads any photos available in your Photo Stream (assuming it is connected to the Internet via a Wi-Fi network of course). Any photos you take with the device's camera after you enable Photo Stream will be uploaded automatically (again, when the device is connected to the Internet via Wi-Fi).

FIGURE 7.2   When Photo Stream is enabled, an iOS device automatically uploads photos you take to the cloud and downloads photos stored there.

TIP: **Another Way to Enable**

You can also enable Photo Stream by moving to the Settings app, tapping **Photos**, and sliding the Photo Stream switch to the ON position.

Viewing Photo Stream Photos on an iOS Device

To view photos stored on your Photo Stream, perform the following steps (which are based on an iPad; iPhone or iPod screens look a bit different, but work in the same way):

1. Tap the **Photos** icon. The app opens.

2. Tap the **Photo Stream** tab (iPad) or tap the **Albums** button and then tap **Photo Stream** (iPhone or iPod touch).

3. Browse the photos stored in your Photo Stream. This works just like browsing photos in other albums on your device. You can drag your finger up or down the screen to scroll all the photos contained there.

4. To view a photo, tap its **thumbnail**. The photo appears on the photo viewer screen, as shown in Figure 7.3.

Working with Photo Stream Photos on an iOS Device

When you tap the Action button (upper-right corner of an iPad screen or lower-left corner on an iPhone or iPod touch), you can perform the following actions on a photo stored in your Photo Stream:

▶ **Email Photo.** Prepares a new email message with the photo attached.

▶ **Message.** Sends the photo to the Messages app where it is attached to a new message that you can send via iMessages or as a text message.

FIGURE 7.3 Viewing a photo from the Photo Stream is just like viewing photos you've take with an iOS device's camera.

▶ **Assign to Contact.** Associates the photo with a contact.

▶ **Use as Wallpaper.** Sets the photo as the wallpaper for your Home screen, the Locked screen, or in both locations.

▶ **Tweet.** Sends the photo via Twitter.

▶ **Print.** Prints the photo on an AirPrint-capable printer.

TIP: **Multiple Photos**

You can perform some of these actions, such as emailing, messaging, or copying, on multiple photos at the same time. When you are browsing the Photo Stream album, tap the **Action** button and then tap each **photo** you want to select. Then tap the **command** you want to use and it will be performed on the selected photos at the same time. For example, if you tap **Email**, the photos you selected are attached to one email message.

▶ **Copy Photo (iPad only).** Copies the photo to the Clipboard so you can paste into other apps.

▶ **Save to Camera Roll.** Saves the photo in the Camera Roll album. This causes the photo to be permanently stored on your iOS device rather than just being stored in your Photo Stream, which is not a permanent location (see the section, "Understanding Photo Stream," earlier in this lesson for details).

NOTE: **iOS Devices without Cameras**

If you use an iPad 1 or an iPod touch 3rd generation, the last command is Save to Saved Photos. It is called Saved Photos because these devices don't have a camera; however, you can save photos attached to emails, received via iMessages, stored in your Photo Stream, and so on.

Saving Photo Stream Photos on an iOS Device

If you don't use Photo Stream with a Mac or a PC, you need to store photos in your Photo Stream that you want to keep in a permanent album. You can do this by saving them to the Camera Roll or Saved Photos album (see the previous section) or by creating an album on the iOS device and saving the photos there.

To create an album on an iOS device and save Photo Stream photos in it, perform the following steps:

1. Open the Photos app.

2. Tap the **Albums** tab.

3. Tap the **Edit** button.

4. Tap **New Album** (iPad) or **Add** (iPhone/iPod touch).

5. Type the name of the album you are creating and tap **Save**, as shown in Figure 7.4. You're prompted to add photos to the new album.

FIGURE 7.4   You can create a photo album on an iOS device and store photos from your Photo Stream there.

6. On an iPad, tap the **Photo Stream** tab or on an iPhone/iPod touch, tap the **Albums** tab and then tap **Photo Stream**.

7. Browse the photos in the Photo Stream.

8. Tap the **photos** you want to save in the new album. Photos you tap are marked with a check mark to show that they are selected, as shown in Figure 7.5.

TIP: **Save Them All**

If you want to save all the photos in your Photo Stream in the new album, tap **Select All Photos** and skip steps 7 through 9.

---

9. Repeat steps 7 and 8 until you've selected all the photos that you want to add to the new album. As you select photos, you see the number currently selected at the top of the screen.

10. Tap **Done**. The new album is created and the photos you selected are stored in it. You can work with the new album just like others you have on your device, and the photos it contains are permanently stored there.

FIGURE 7.5   Photos you are adding to the album are marked with a check mark.

To store photos from your Photo Stream in an album that already exists (such as the one you created with the previous steps), perform the following steps:

1. Open the Photos app.

2. Tap the **Albums** tab.

3. On an iPad, tap the **Photo Stream** tab or on an iPhone/iPod touch, tap the **Albums** tab and then tap **Photo Stream**.

4. Tap the **Action** button (upper-right corner of the screen).

5. Browse the photos in the Photo Stream.

6. Tap the **photos** you want to save in an album. Photos you tap are marked with a check mark to show that they are selected. As you tap photos, the number of photos you have selected is shown at the top of the screen.

7. Tap **Add To**. You're prompted to choose an existing album or to create a new album and add the selected photos to it (this works similarly to the previous set of steps).

NOTE: **Save Versus Add To**

If you tap **Save,** the selected photos are saved in the Camera Roll or Saved Photos (iPad 1 or iPod touch 3rd generation) albums whereas **Add To** enables you to choose the location in which you want to save the photos.

---

8. Tap **Add to Existing Album**. You move to the Albums tab where you see all the albums in the Photos app. Albums you created on the device are highlighted while albums coming from other sources are grayed out (this is more visible on iPads than on iPhones/iPod touches). This is because you can only move photos to albums created on the device. The number of photos you are moving along with a thumbnail are shown at the top of the screen, as shown in Figure 7.6.

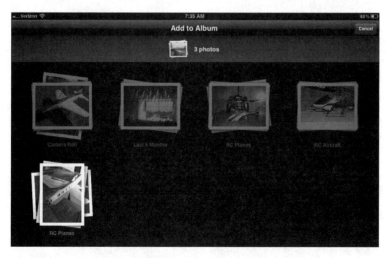

FIGURE 7.6   Tap an album to store photos you have selected there.

9. Tap the **album** in which you want to store the photos. The selected photos are stored in the album and you return to the Photo Stream. This saves the photos in that location so they remain even after they are removed from the Photo Stream.

Using Photo Stream with a Mac

Photo Stream works great with a Mac. Like other devices, you need to first enable Photo Stream on the Mac. Then, you can work with your Photo Stream photos in either iPhoto or Aperture. Both applications automatically download and save all your Photo Stream photos, and of course you can edit them, save them in albums, use them in projects, and all the other great tasks you can do with any of your other photos stored in those applications.

> NOTE: **Mac Requirements**
> To use Photo Stream on a Mac, your Mac must be running OS X Lion 10.7.2 or later. Photo Stream is compatible with iPhoto 9.2 or later and Aperture 3.2 or later.

Enabling Photo Stream on a Mac

To enable Photo Stream on a Mac, perform the following steps:

1. Open the System Preferences application.

2. Click **iCloud**. The iCloud pane appears.

3. Check the **Photo Stream** check box, as shown in Figure 7.7. Photo Stream becomes available in iPhoto or Aperture and is ready to use in those applications.

> NOTE: **One Application at a Time**
> You can use Photo Stream in only one application at a time. If you are already using Photo Stream in iPhoto and try to use it in Aperture (or vice versa), you're prompted to change the application that accesses your Photo Stream. Also, photos are only

downloaded from Photo Stream once. If you have downloaded all your Photo Stream photos into one application, such as iPhoto, and then switch to the other one, namely Aperture, only photos added to your Photo Stream after you make the switch are automatically downloaded to the current application.

FIGURE 7.7   Enabling Photo Stream on a Mac requires just a few clicks.

Using Photo Stream with iPhoto

After you've enabled Photo Stream on your Mac, you can access it in the iPhoto application:

1. Launch iPhoto.

2. Click **Photo Stream** on the Source list. You're prompted to enable Photo Stream, as shown in Figure 7.8.

3. Click **Turn On Photo Stream**. iPhoto starts Photo Stream and downloads the photos currently stored there. Photos added there over time are automatically downloaded as well. When you add photos to iPhoto from other sources, such as importing them from a digital camera, they are uploaded to Photo Stream, too.

FIGURE 7.8   In iPhoto, enable Photo Stream to cause iPhoto to download all the photos stored there.

As you work with Photo Stream and iPhoto, keep the following points in mind:

▶ You don't have to move photos from the Photo Stream to your iPhoto Library to store them on your Mac. This happens automatically when iPhoto downloads photos from the Photo Stream. You can view the Photo Stream photos stored on your Mac by selecting Photos or any of the other sources in the Library. After they are downloaded from Photo Stream, you can use all of iPhoto's tools on them, just like photos you've added from other sources.

▶ If there are a lot of photos in your Photo Stream when you first enable it in iPhoto, it can take a while for all of the photos to be downloaded to your Mac.

▶ To see the photos in your Photo Stream, select it on the Source list, as shown in Figure 7.9. You can browse and view the photos here just like other sources. Though, since the photos are

automatically stored in your iPhoto Library, there isn't a lot of
reason to work with the Photo Stream source; just work with the
photos in the other sources that are stored on your Mac instead.

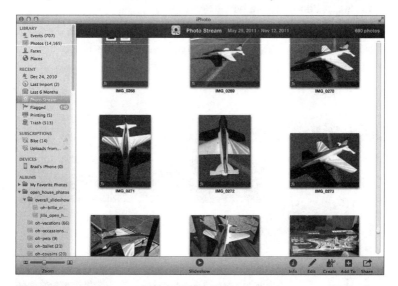

FIGURE 7.9   When you select the Photo Stream source, you see all the
photos stored there, which can be up to 1,000 of them.

▶ iPhoto periodically and automatically updates the Photo Stream
   source. When this happens, you see the updating icon (a rotating
   circle made up of two curved arrows) next to the Photo Stream
   icon on the Source list. iPhoto updates the Photo Stream each
   time you launch the application, too.

Using Photo Stream with Aperture

Apple's Aperture photo application also supports Photo Stream. It automatically downloads photos from your Photo Stream and uploads photos
you add to your Aperture Library from other sources, such as a camera.

Like iPhoto, you need to enable your Photo Stream in Aperture:

1. Launch Aperture.

2. Select **Photo Stream** on the Source list.

3. Click **Turn On Photo Stream**, as shown in Figure 7.10. Aperture begins downloading the photos from your Photo Stream. As it downloads photos, it stores them in your Aperture Library.

FIGURE 7.10   You can enable Aperture to automatically access your Photo Stream.

After Photo Stream is enabled, you can select it on the Source list to view the photos there, as shown in Figure 7.11. Like iPhoto, since the Photo Stream photos are automatically stored in your Library, you can work with them there rather than in the Photo Stream, but you can always see what's currently in your Photo Stream if that is of interest to you.

FIGURE 7.11   When you select Photo Stream in Aperture, you see the photos in your Photo Stream.

TIP: **Downloading Manually**

You can manually download photos from your Photo Stream into either iPhoto or Aperture. Just select and browse the Photo Stream source. Drag photos from that source onto the Library. The downloaded photos are added to the Library. You can re-download photos as many times as you'd like while they remain in your Photo Stream.

CAUTION: **Photo Stream and Disk Space**

As you've learned, when you use Photo Stream with a Mac or a Windows PC, photos are automatically downloaded and stored on your computer. You save time since manual syncing is not required. However, it also means that *every* photo you take with Photo Stream-enabled devices is permanently stored on your computer. If you take a lot of photos, this can consume a large amount of disk space. You should establish a habit of regularly "pruning" the photos downloaded from Photo Stream to your computer to remove photos that you don't want to keep. You should also use your photo application to tag downloaded photos so that you can keep them organized and easy to find.

Using Photo Stream with a Windows PC

When you use Photo Stream with a Windows PC, photos are automatically downloaded to a folder you designate and uploaded from a folder you select. Like other devices, you first enable Photo Stream and then you can take advantage of the automatic photo downloads and uploads.

NOTE: **Windows PC Requirements**

To use Photo Stream on a Windows PC, you must run Windows 7 or Windows Vista (Service Pack 2) and have the iCloud Control Panel for Windows installed. (The information in this section is based on Windows 7.)

Enabling Photo Stream on a Windows PC

To start using Photo Stream on a Windows PC, enable it with the following steps:

1. Open the iCloud control panel.

2. Check the **Photo Stream** check box.

3. Click **Options**. The Photo Stream Options dialog appears, as shown in Figure 7.12; you use this to designate the Photo Stream download and upload folders.

4. To select the folder to which you want your Photo Stream photos downloaded, click the upper **Change** button, choose the folder you want your photos to be downloaded to automatically, and click **OK**. You can leave the default location selected, which is in your Pictures folder.

FIGURE 7.12   Use the iCloud control panel to enable Photo Stream.

5. To select the folder from which you want your Photo Stream photos uploaded, click the lower **Change** button, choose the folder you want your photos to be downloaded to automatically, and click **OK**. You can leave the default location selected, which is in your Pictures folder.

6. Click **OK**. The Photo Stream Options dialog closes.

7. Click **Apply** or **Close**. The photos in your Photo Stream are downloaded to your computer; if any photos are in your upload folder, they are uploaded to your Photo Stream.

Using Photo Stream Photos on a Windows PC

After you configure Photo Stream on your PC, you can access the photos it downloads by opening the folder you configured in the previous step 4.

Open that folder to see the photos that have been downloaded from your Photo Stream, as shown in Figure 7.13. You can use these photos just like any others on your computer. For example, you can import them into a photo application such as Adobe Photoshop Organizer.

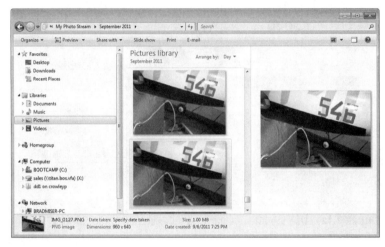

FIGURE 7.13   Photos in your Photo Stream are automatically downloaded to the selected folder.

To upload photos to your Photo Stream, just place them in the folder you selected in the previous step 5. They are uploaded to your Photo Stream and then downloaded to any other devices that access your Photo Stream.

NOTE: **No Windows Apps...Yet**

At press time, there weren't any Windows PC photo apps that support Photo Stream as iPhoto and Aperture for the Mac do. However, given the popularity of iOS devices, one might be available as you are reading this. If you use a Windows PC, do a web search for Windows photo application and Photo Stream. Hopefully, you'll find an application that supports Photo Stream to make Photo Stream even more useful to you.

Using Photo Stream with an Apple TV

An Apple TV is a great way to view your photos. Prior to Photo Stream, you had to sync your photos to some other device to be able to view them using an Apple TV. With Photo Stream, you can view photos on your Apple TV automatically.

> **NOTE: Apple TV 2 or Later**
> To use Photo Stream with an Apple TV, it must be version 2 or later running Software Update version 4.4 or later.

Enabling Photo Stream on an Apple TV

To enable photo stream,

1. Start up the Apple TV.

2. Select the **Internet** menu.

3. Select **Photo Stream**.

4. If you've already configured your iCloud account on the Apple TV, select **Yes**; if you want to use a different account, select **No, use a different account** and follow the prompts to enter the account you want to use. The Apple TV connects to your account.

5. If you want your Photo Stream to be your Apple TV's screen saver, select **Yes**; if you want to keep the current screen saver, select **No**. You move to the Photo Stream screen and your photos start to download. The amount of time it takes to download all of them depends upon the number of photos you have and your connection speed. You can start viewing photos as others download.

Viewing Your Photo Stream on an Apple TV

To view your Photo Stream, select **Internet**, **Photo Stream**. You move to the Photo Stream screen and see thumbnails for all the photos in your Photo Stream. Here, you can do the following:

- ► You can use the remote to browse the thumbnails.

- ► To see a photo at full size, select its **thumbnail**; you move to the next or previous photo using the remote. Press **menu** on the remote to move back to the Photo Stream screen.

- ► To configure how the photos play in a slideshow, select **Settings**. On this screen, you can configure how photos in the slideshow are presented (such as shuffle, repeat), choose the music (the playlist) you want to hear while the slideshow plays, and the slideshow's theme.

- ► To view the photos in a sideshow select **Slideshow** or just press the **Play** button. The slideshow plays according to the settings; for example, if you configured music, you hear that music while the slideshow plays.

Removing Photos from Your Photo Stream

Photos remain in your Photo Stream for 30 days. After that time, they are deleted automatically. Since photos don't count against your iCloud storage space, you don't really need to delete photos from your Photo Stream. However, if you want to remove your photos from your Photo Stream for some other reason, you can do so. There are two steps to this process. First, delete the photos from the Photo Stream on the cloud. Second, delete the photos from the Photo Stream on each device on which they appear.

CAUTION: **Not So Fast**

Don't delete photos from your Photo Stream on the cloud or from your devices unless your sure you don't want those photos. If you do want some of them, make sure they exist in a permanent location on your computer or iOS devices before deleting them from the cloud or from individual devices.

To remove photos from your Photo Stream on the cloud, perform the following steps:

1. Log into your iCloud website.

2. Click on **your name** in the upper-right corner of the window. The Account pane appears.

3. Click **Advanced**.

4. Click **Reset Photo Stream**.

5. At the prompt, click **Reset**. All the photos in your Photo Stream are removed immediately.

To remove Photo Stream photos from your devices, follow the steps in the corresponding bullet to remove them from each device:

▶ **iOS Devices.** Open the Settings app and tap **iCloud**. Tap **Photo Stream**. Slide the Photo Stream slider to the OFF position. The photos in the Photo Stream album are deleted and photos are no longer downloaded automatically.

▶ **Macs.** Disable Photo Stream in iPhoto or Aperture; this removes Photo Stream from those applications. Also disable Photo Stream on the iCloud pane of the System Preferences application. If photos were automatically downloaded from Photo Stream and you don't want them on your computer any more, you also need to delete them from the iPhoto or Aperture Library.

▶ **Windows PCs.** Disable Photo Stream on the iCloud control panel by unchecking its check box. If you don't want any of the photos that were automatically downloaded from Photo Stream to remain on your PC, open the Download folder and delete the photos inside. If you imported photos into a photo application, you need to delete them from there as well.

> NOTE: **Photo Streaming Again**
> You can start using Photo Stream again at any time by simply re-configuring it using the sections in this lesson. If you've removed all the photos from your Photo Stream, you'll start with a clean slate—or should I say stream?

Summary

In this lesson, you learned how to use Photo Stream to make your photos available on your iOS devices, Macintoshes, or Windows PCs. In the next lesson, you learn how to use iCloud with your documents.

LESSON 8

Using iCloud with Your Documents

In this lesson, you learn how to use iCloud to work with the same documents on iOS devices, Macs, and Windows PCs. You also learn about the iWork area of your iCloud website.

Syncing Documents with iCloud

Creating, editing, and producing documents, such as text, spreadsheets, presentations, and so on, are one of the primary reasons computers and related devices are so incredibly useful. When you work on the same documents on different devices, it can be a real pain to make sure you are working with the most recent version of your documents on each device. There are lots of ways to do this, from storing documents in folders that get synced on your devices to emailing them to yourself, but all of those approaches have their drawbacks. As you can probably guess from the title of this lesson, iCloud can help you with this chore.

iCloud offers automatic and nearly instantaneous syncing of your documents on iOS devices, somewhat automated syncing on Macs, and manual syncing on Windows PCs. It does this by storing your documents in the iWork area of your iCloud website. From there, all the documents you sync are available to iOS devices, Macs, and Windows PCs.

The reason there are different levels of syncing on each type of device is that, as of press time, iCloud syncing is only supported natively for documents in the iOS versions of the iWork apps (Pages for word processing, Numbers for spreadsheets, and Keynote for presentations). On the Mac, you can use documents you sync in the Mac versions of the iWork applications (also Pages, Numbers, and Keynote), but the syncing process itself isn't automatic because you have to download and upload the documents on which you work. On a Windows PC, the process is even less streamlined because you have to use different applications altogether because there aren't Windows versions of the iWork applications. (iCloud syncing does support downloading documents in the MS Office formats.)

Because of these complexities, iCloud document syncing is currently a bit of a mixed bag. If you work extensively on documents on different iOS devices, you'll probably find it to be very useful. If you work on documents on both iOS devices and Macs, you'll probably find it to be a good way to keep your documents in sync though not as slick as for iOS devices. If you share documents on a Windows PC, the sync process is a bit more cumbersome but still might be useful.

In this lesson, you find information about using document syncing with each type of device. You might just need to try using it for your own documents to see how useful it is to you based on the types of devices and applications you use most.

NOTE: **Predicting the Future of iCloud Document Syncing**

Although I don't have information from Apple, I can speculate on the future of iCloud document syncing. It seems highly likely that in the near future, Apple will update the Mac versions of the iWork applications to support seamless iCloud syncing; syncing documents on a Mac would work just like syncing on iOS devices does today. Also, Apple has made the tools needed to enable iCloud document syncing available to software developers. This enables them to add support for iCloud document syncing to their applications. It's likely that many applications will eventually offer iCloud syncing, given the incredible popularity of iOS devices. (For example, there are credible rumors that MS Office will support iCloud document syncing natively and that iOS versions of the Office applications are in the works.) If you use this aspect of iCloud, keep your ears and eyes open for future developments.

Syncing Documents on iOS Devices

After you have configured your iCloud account on an iOS device as explained in Lesson 2, "Configuring iCloud on an iPhone, iPod touch, or

iPad," you need to ensure that document syncing is enabled for your
iCloud account on each device with which you want to sync documents.
You can also determine which apps use iCloud document syncing. When
enabled, you can use apps that support iCloud syncing to access the same
documents on any of your iOS devices.

Enabling Document Syncing on iOS Devices

To enable an iOS device to sync documents, perform the following steps:

1. Open the Settings app.

2. Tap **iCloud**.

3. Tap **Documents & Data**.

4. Set the **Documents & Data** switch to ON, as shown in Figure
   8.1. This configures the device to use iCloud to store documents
   in the cloud so that you can sync them on your devices.

FIGURE 8.1   Set the Documents & Data switch to the ON position to store
documents on which you work in the cloud.

5. If you are configuring a device that supports a cellular data network, set the **Use Cellular** switch to ON if you want document
   syncing to occur when you are using the cellular network or to
   OFF if you only want document syncing to occur when you are
   using a Wi-Fi network. If your cellular data account has a limit
   on the amount of data you can transfer, you might want to leave
   this in the OFF position so that document syncing doesn't use up
   a significant portion of your monthly data allotment or result in
   overage charges (which can be very expensive).

> TIP: **Temp Syncing**
> If you do disable the Use Cellular setting and are working on a doc-ument while you only have access to your cellular network, you can always go back to the Documents & Data screen and temporarily enable cellular syncing to ensure the document gets copied to the cloud. Then, turn it OFF again so that you don't use up your monthly data allotment or you might get hit with overage charges.

Enabling Document Syncing in iOS Apps

In addition to enabling iCloud document syncing at the device level, you must also enable or disable this feature for each app you use. There are two ways in which document syncing can be enabled for iOS apps.

The first time you launch an app, you're prompted to store your documents, as shown in Figure 8.2. Tap **Use iCloud** to enable document syncing.

FIGURE 8.2   When you launch an iOS app for the first time, you're prompted to enable iCloud document syncing.

> **NOTE: iWork Apps Only**
>
> As mentioned previously, when this book was written, only Apple's iWork apps supported iCloud document syncing. However, as other apps add this support, it is likely to work very similarly for them as well.

You can enable or disable iCloud document syncing at any time by opening the Settings app and tapping the **icon** for the app you want to configure; for example, tap **Pages** to enable or disable document syncing for the Pages app. On the app's Setting screen, set the **Use iCloud** switch to the ON position to enable document syncing, as shown in Figure 8.3; or set it in the OFF position if you only want the documents to be stored on the device.

FIGURE 8.3   iCloud document syncing is enabled for the Pages app.

When iCloud document syncing is enabled, any documents with which you are working and any documents you create are automatically stored on the cloud. On the cloud, they are stored with documents created on other devices that also have iCloud document syncing enabled for the same apps.

Working with Synced Documents on iOS Devices

Any iOS apps documents that are stored on the cloud are automatically available in apps for which iCloud document syncing is enabled. When you open the document management area of the app, you see all its documents that are on the cloud, as shown in Figure 8.4.

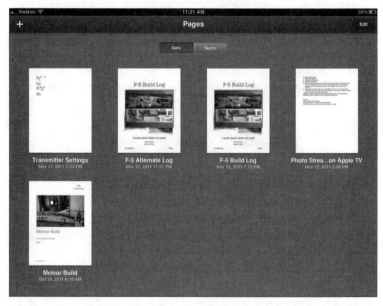

FIGURE 8.4   Documents stored on the cloud are shown on the document management screen in iOS apps (Pages in this case).

To work with a document, tap it. It opens in the app, and you can edit it as you normally would. The following are some other aspects of iCloud syncing that might help you work with it more effectively:

▶ When a document needs to be updated (on the cloud), its icon has a folded corner, as shown in Figure 8.5. Modified documents are uploaded automatically so you don't need to take action; this lets you know that you should let the upload process happen before working with the document on other devices.

FIGURE 8.5 This document has been modified and needs to be uploaded to the cloud. (This iPad is currently not connected to the Internet.)

▶ As documents are uploaded, you see progress bars in the documents' icons and a status message in the upper-right corner of the screen (which shows how many documents are being updated). When the progress bar disappears, the documents are available on the cloud and are available on other synced devices.

▶ It's possible for the versions of a document to get out of sync if it is being edited on two different devices at the same time. This can also happen if you work on a document using a device that isn't connected to the Internet and then work on the same document on a second device. When you reconnect the first device, iCloud won't know which version it should use as the master. Whenever there is a conflict between versions of a document, you are presented with a dialog, as shown in Figure 8.6, that enables you to choose the version you want to use as the master for that document. Tap the version you want to keep and then tap **Keep**. The version you selected becomes the master version stored on the cloud and subsequently is available on other synced devices.

FIGURE 8.6   When there is a conflict over versions of documents, you can choose which version you want to become the master.

iCloud document syncing works very well with iOS apps; in fact, most of the time, it will be transparent to you, which is exactly how you want syncing to work. You don't even have to think about it because the iCloud service manages the process for you.

Using the iWork Feature of Your iCloud Website

As you learned in Lesson 1, "Getting Started with Your iCloud Account and Website," your iCloud account includes a website that has applications you can use. One of these is the iWork area, which is where you access documents directly on the cloud. To use iCloud document syncing with Macs or Windows PCs, you need to download or upload documents you want to sync via your website.

To access your documents, perform the following steps (if you need help, refer to Lesson 1):

1. Log into your iCloud website.

2. Open the iWork application.

3. Click the application tab for the documents with which you want
to work, such as **Keynote**, **Pages**, or **Numbers**. (In the future,
there may be additional options as more applications support
iCloud document syncing.) You see the documents from the
application that are stored in the cloud, as shown in Figure 8.7.

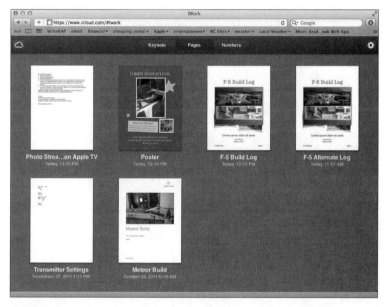

FIGURE 8.7   You can use your iCloud website to access your documents on
the cloud.

4. Select the document with which you want to work or select a
command on the menu that appears when you click the **Action**
(gear) button.

When a document is selected, open the Action menu to do any of the
following:

▶ Choose **Download Document** to download it to a computer. In
the resulting dialog, choose the file format in which you want the
document downloaded; choose the option that matches the application you're going to use to work with the document on the

computer. The options you see depends on the type of document you selected. Figure 8.8 shows the options for Pages document. What happens after you download the document depends on the format you selected and the type of computer you use to download it (the options are explained in the following sections).

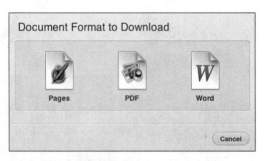

FIGURE 8.8   These format options are visible when you download a Pages document.

▶ Choose **Delete Document** to remove it from your website.

CAUTION: **Deleting Documents**
When you delete a document from your website, it is also deleted from any iOS devices. If you want to keep a version of the document, download it to a computer before you delete it.

▶ Choose **Duplicate Document** to create a copy. Copies you create become available on synced iOS devices too.

You can also upload documents to the cloud from a Mac or Windows PC, which is required for them to be available on your iOS devices. On the Action menu, choose **Upload Document**. Move to and select the document you want to upload. Press the **Return** key (Mac) or **Enter** key (Windows). The document is uploaded to your website. You can use the progress dialog that appears, as shown in Figure 8.9, to monitor the process. When the process finishes, you see the document on your website, and it is also synced on your iOS devices.

FIGURE 8.9 Upload your documents to the cloud to make them available on other devices.

> TIP: **Drag and Drop Uploading**
> You can also upload a document by dragging it from your desktop and dropping it onto the iCloud website window.

Syncing Documents on Macs

You can use your iCloud website to keep documents in sync on your Mac, iOS devices, and Windows PCs. Currently, on a Mac, the sync process is manual (unlike on iOS devices), but by using the iCloud website, it is not difficult or time-consuming.

Configuring Document Syncing on a Mac

To use iCloud document syncing on a Mac, ensure that your iCloud account is set to sync documents by performing the following steps:

1. Open the System Preferences application.

2. Click the **iCloud** icon. The iCloud pane appears.

3. Ensure the **Documents & Data** check box is checked, as shown in Figure 8.10.

FIGURE 8.10   Check the Documents & Data check box to sync your documents on a Mac.

Working with iCloud Document Syncing on a Mac

In the previous section, "Using the iWork Feature of Your iCloud Website," you pretty much learned everything you need to know to use iCloud to sync documents on your Mac.

When you are ready to work on a document, download it from your website as follows:

1. Move to the iWork area of your iCloud website.

TIP: **More Convenient Document Syncing**

To make syncing documents more convenient, open a separate web browser window and move to your iWork area. When you log into iCloud, make sure you check the check box so you remain signed in. Leave the iWork window open at all times (you can minimize to the Dock to move it out of your way or use Mission Control to add it to a desktop space). This way, you can just jump into the window to download or upload documents. This saves a few clicks because you only have to do this when you log out of or restart your Mac.

---

2. Click the tab for the type of document you want to work with, such as **Keynote**, **Pages**, or **Numbers**.

3. Click the document you want to use.

4. Click **Download**.

5. Click the file format you want; the options depend on the type of document you are working with. For example, if you selected Numbers in step 2, the options are **Numbers**, **PDF**, or **Excel**, as shown in Figure 8.11. iCloud prepares the file and then downloads it. After the file downloads, it opens in the application associated with the file type you downloaded (for example, if you selected the Numbers format, the file opens in the Numbers application).

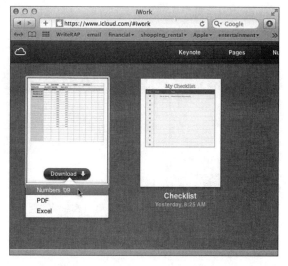

FIGURE 8.11 When you download a spreadsheet, you can choose Numbers, PDF, or Excel depending on the application you want to use with the document.

6. Use the application to work with the document.

NOTE: **Where'd It Go?**

When you download a document from iCloud, it is stored in your designated download folder, which is the Downloads folder in your Home folder by default. To see the current download folder, open your browser's Preferences and see where it downloads files. (In Safari, this is on the General tab of the Preferences dialog.)

When you finish working with a document, you need to upload it to your iCloud website so it is synced to your iOS devices and becomes available to download onto other computers.

To upload the document, perform the following steps:

1. Move your iCloud web window so that it is visible on the desktop.

2. Click the tab for the type of document you are uploading, such as **Keynote**, **Pages**, or **Numbers**.

3. Drag the file from your desktop onto the web window, as shown in Figure 8.12.

FIGURE 8.12   To upload a document on which you've worked, drag it from the desktop onto the iWork page.

4. If you've previously downloaded the document and want to replace the version on the website with the version you modified, click **Replace**. The updated file is stored in your iWork area, where it is copied onto synced iOS devices (the next time you

open the associated app), and is available to be downloaded to other computers. (If you want to store a different version on the website instead, click **Cancel**, rename the file, and upload it again.)

> NOTE: **Your Action Required**
>
> After you modify a document on your Mac, don't forget to upload the revised version to your iCloud website. This is a bit of a nuisance, but if you get into the habit of moving documents onto your website when you're done working with them, it's less likely you'll end up using an outdated version on another device.

As of this writing, the Mac versions of the iWork applications actually use a different file format than the iOS versions. Because of this, you might see some messages about various elements of the file not being supported when you open files you've modified on a Mac in an iOS app. Until the applications are updated to support the same features, you just have to deal with the differences as you are notified about them.

> NOTE: **The Secret Sync Folder**
>
> Documents you sync with iCloud are managed through a folder in your Library folder, which is hidden by default. To see this folder, hold the option key down, open the Go menu, and choose **Library**. In this folder, you see the Mobile Documents folder. Inside this folder, you see a folder for each file type, such as Keynote, Numbers, and Pages. You can actually add documents to your iCloud website by placing them within the Documents folders within each file type's folder. However, when you do this, each file is recognized as a different version, so if you had a previous version of the file on your website, the version you place in this folder is added to the website but doesn't replace this version. You can also access files within these folders, but because the file types are different, you can't just double-click a file to open it. For these reasons, it is recommended you don't use these folders. Hopefully, Apple will make the syncing process more automatic so that documents can be transferred to and from the website by placing them in specific folders; until then, working with the website gives the best results.

Syncing Documents on Windows PCs

In the earlier section, "Using the iWork Feature of Your iCloud Website," you pretty much learned everything you need to know to use iCloud to sync documents on your Windows PC.

There are two steps you need to do to sync your documents. When you are ready to work on a document, download it to your computer. When you've finished working on it, upload it to your iCloud website so it is available to other devices.

To download a document, do the following steps:

1. Move to the iWork area of your iCloud website.

TIP: **More Convenient Document Syncing**

To make syncing documents more convenient, open a separate web browser window and move to your iWork area. When you log into iCloud, make sure you check the check box so you remain signed in. Leave the iWork window open at all times (you can minimize the window to move it out of your way). This way, you can just jump into the window to download or upload documents. This saves a few clicks because you only have to do this when you log out of or restart your computer.

---

2. Click the tab for the type of document you want to work with, such as **Keynote**, **Pages**, or **Numbers**.

3. Click the **document** you want to use.

4. Click **Download**.

5. Click the file format you want; the options depend on the type of document you are working with. For example, if you selected Pages in step 2, the options are **Pages**, **PDF**, or **Word**. iCloud prepares the file. When that process is complete, you're prompted to download the file.

6. Click the **Download** button, as shown in Figure 8.13. After the file starts to download, you're prompted to open or save it.

Creating a file for download.

F-5 Build Log

Cancel   Download

FIGURE 8.13   A Pages file is downloaded in the Word format.

7. Click **Save**.

8. Choose the location where you want to save the file and click **Save**. The document is saved to the location you selected.

9. When the save process is complete, click **Open**. The document opens in the association application.

10. Use the application to work with the document.

Because there aren't Windows versions of the iWork apps, you might have to deal with some issues related to working with iWork files in Office applications, but hopefully these won't be too difficult to deal with.

When you're done working with a document, you need to upload it to your iCloud website so it will be synced to your iOS devices and available to download onto other computers.

To upload the document, perform the following steps:

1. Move your iCloud web window so that it is visible on the desktop.

2. Click the tab for the type of document you are uploading, such as **Keynote**, **Pages**, or **Numbers**.

3. Drag the file from your desktop onto the web window.

4. If you've previously downloaded the document and want to replace the version on the website with the version you modified, click **Replace**. The updated file is stored in your iWork area from where it is copied onto synced iOS devices (the next time you open the associated app) and is available to be downloaded to other computers. (If you want to store a different version on the website instead, click Cancel, rename the file, and upload it again.)

NOTE: **Can't Upload?**

If you receive an error message when you try to upload a document, the file type you are trying to upload probably isn't supported or you might not have the correct tab selected (such as Keynote for presentations).

Summary

In this lesson, you learned how to use your iCloud account to sync documents on your devices. In the next lesson, you learn how to use iCloud for email.

LESSON 9

Configuring Your iCloud Email

In this lesson, you learn how to configure your devices to work with your iCloud email and to use the iCloud email web application.

Working with iCloud Email

An iCloud account includes email service, which you can sync across iOS devices, Macintosh computers, and Windows PCs. You can also work with your iCloud email using the email application available on your iCloud website; this enables you to use your iCloud email on any device that has a compatible web browser and Internet connection.

Your iCloud email address is the Apple ID associated with your iCloud account. In most cases, this is something like *youraccountname*@me.com, where *youraccountname* is the name you chose when you created your Apple ID account.

This lesson explains how to configure iCloud email on each type of device. iCloud email is designed to work in the Mail app on iOS devices, in Mail on Macintosh computers, and in Outlook on Windows PCs. You can also set up other applications to work with your iCloud email account in the event you don't want to use one of the default email applications.

Setting Up iCloud Email on iOS Devices

Assuming you've already configured your iCloud account on an iOS device as explained in Lesson 2, "Configuring iCloud on an iPhone, iPod touch, or iPad," you need to ensure that Mail is enabled for your iCloud account. You can also configure other options for your iCloud email.

Enabling iCloud Email on an iOS Device

Open the Settings app, tap iCloud and ensure the Mail switch is set to the ON position, as shown in Figure 9.1. This configures the Mail app to use your iCloud email account.

FIGURE 9.1   Set the Mail switch to the ON position to activate your iCloud email account in the Mail app.

That's all you have to do to start using your iCloud email account in the Mail app. When you open the Mail app, you see your iCloud account listed on the Mailboxes screen, as shown in Figure 9.2. You can tap the **iCloud inbox** to view your iCloud messages or tap All Inboxes to see the messages in all your accounts. To work with your iCloud email account folders, tap **iCloud** in the Accounts section. (Of course, if you changed your iCloud account's description, the description you created appears instead of "iCloud.")

NOTE: **One and Only Account?**
If your iCloud email account is the only one enabled on your device, you see the folders for your iCloud email account on the Mailboxes screen. You tap any of the listed folders to access them. For example, to see your messages, tap **Inbox**.

FIGURE 9.2   When you enable your iCloud email account, it appears in the Mail app.

Determining How iCloud Email Is Synced on an iOS Device

As you learned in Lesson 2, you can configure how and how often iCloud information is updated on your iOS device. For iCloud email, you have three options: Push, Fetch, or Manual (see Lesson 2 for an explanation of these options). To determine how your iCloud email information is synced, follow these steps:

1. Open the Settings app.

2. Tap **Mail, Contacts, Calendars**.

3. Tap **Fetch New Data**.

4. Tap **Advanced**.

5. Tap **your iCloud account**.

6. Tap **Push**, **Fetch**, or **Manual**. Your iCloud email is synced on the device according to the setting you select. If you select Manual, open the Mail app to sync your email.

> NOTE: **Don't Push Me!**
> Even if you disable Push on the Fetch New Data screen, the Push option is available for your iCloud email. However, if you select it, email is synced using Fetch as long as Push is disabled on your device.

Changing Global Email Settings on an iOS Device

To make changes that impact all of your email accounts (not just your iCloud email account), complete the following steps:

1. Move to the Mail, Contacts, Calendars screen.

2. If necessary, scroll down until you see the Mail section.

3. Tap **Show**.

4. Tap the number of recent messages you want to display in the Mail app.

5. Tap the Return button (which is labeled **Mail...** on iPhones or iPod touches or **Mail, Contacts...** on an iPad).

6. Tap **Preview**.

7. Tap the number of lines you want to display for each email message when you view the inbox. This enables you to read part of the message without opening it.

8. Tap the **Return** button.

9. Tap **Minimum Font Size**.

10. Tap the smallest font size you want to use for email. The larger the size, the easier to read, but the less information fits on a single screen.

11. Tap the **Return** button.

12. Set the **Show To/Cc Label** slider to ON to always see the To and Cc labels in email headers. (With this disabled, you can view this information on a message by tapping Details.)

13. If you don't want to confirm your action when you delete messages, set the **Ask Before Deleting** switch to OFF. When you delete a message, it immediately goes into the trash.

14. If you want images in HTML email messages to be displayed automatically when you read messages, set the **Load Remote Images** switch to ON. If you disable this by setting it to OFF, you can manually load images in a message. If you receive a lot of spam, you should disable this so that you won't see images in which you might not be interested and to avoid any chance that images can be used to validate your email address.

15. If you don't want Mail to organize your messages by thread (which means grouping them based on their subjects so that you see all the messages on a single topic on the same screen), disable this feature by setting the **Organize by Thread** slider to OFF. With this setting disabled, messages are listed individually in your Inbox. With this setting enabled, messages on the same topic are grouped together.

16. If you don't want to receive a blind copy of each email you send, set **Always Bcc Myself** to OFF. If you set the status to ON, each time you send a message, you also receive a copy of it, but your address is not shown to the message's other recipients.

17. Tap **Increase Quote Level**.

18. If you don't want Mail to automatically indent current content (quoted content) when you reply or forward email, slide the **Increase Quote Level** switch to OFF. Generally, you should leave this enabled (ON) so it is easier for the recipients to tell when you have added content versus that quoted content.

19. Tap the **Return** button.

20. Tap **Signature**.

21. Enter the signature you want to append to each message you
     send. If you don't want an automatic signature, delete all the text
     on the screen. You can include links or graphics in your signature
     by either typing them in or pasting them, as shown in Figure 9.3.

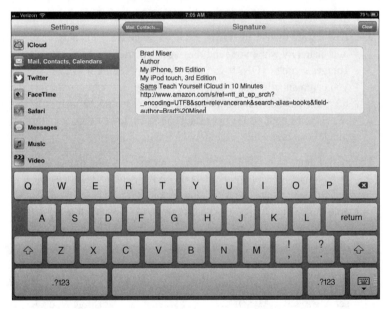

FIGURE 9.3   You can configure a signature that is automatically added to
your email messages.

22. Tap the **Return** button.

23. Tap **Default Account**.

24. Tap the **account** you want to be your default. The default account
     appears at the top of lists and is used as the From address for
     emails you create as new messages. (Of course, you can change
     the From address on messages when you create them.) It is also
     the one used when you send photos, YouTube videos, and so on.

25. Tap the **Return** button. You have completed configuring the functional aspects of the Mail app, as shown in Figure 9.4.

FIGURE 9.4   Use the Mail, Contacts, Calendars screen to configure email options.

You can also configure how you are notified when mail actions happen. Notifications can be audible and visible.

To set the audible notifications, do the following:

1. Move into the Settings app if you aren't there already.

2. On an iPhone or iPad, tap **Sounds**; if you are using an iPad, tap **General** and then **Sounds**.

3. Tap **New Mail**.

4. Tap the **sound** you want to play when you receive new mail or tap **None** if you don't want a sound to play. When you tap a sound, you hear it, and it is marked with a check mark showing you it is the selected sound.

5. Tap **Sounds**.

6. Tap **Sent Mail**.

7. Tap the **sound** you want to play when you send mail or tap **None** if you don't want a sound to play.

To set the visible email notifications, do the following:

1. Move into the Settings app if you aren't there already.

2. Tap **Notifications**.

3. Tap **Mail**. You see the Mail notifications screen, as shown in Figure 9.5.

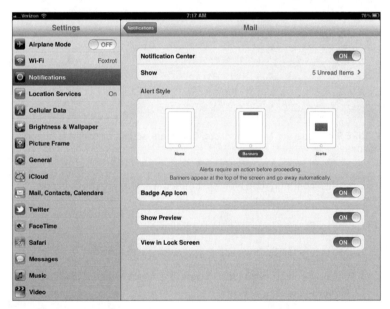

FIGURE 9.5 Use this screen to configure how you want to be notified of email activity.

4. To have email information included on the Notification Center (which opens when you swipe down from the top of the screen), set **Notification Center** to ON. If you don't want this, leave it set to OFF and skip to step 8.

5. Tap **Show**.

6. Tap the number of unread messages that you want to be displayed in the Notification Center.

7. Tap **Mail**.

8. Tap the **Alert Style** for new email messages. The options are

   ▶ **None.** No notifications are displayed when you receive new message.

   ▶ **Banners.** Banners appear at the top of the screen. You see the sender and subject for the new message. You can tap the message to open it in Mail, or do nothing and the banner rotates off the screen in a few seconds.

   ▶ **Alerts.** Alerts appear in the center of the screen. You see the message's sender and subject. You can tap the Dismiss button to remove the alert or the Read button to read the message. You must do one or the other to remove the alert from the screen.

9. To see a counter on the Mail icon showing how many new email messages you have received, set the **Badge App Icon** slider to the ON position. If you set this to OFF, the counter doesn't appear.

10. To include a preview of the message on the Notification Center or Lock screen, set the **Show Preview** setting to ON.

11. To see new email message notifications when your device is locked, set the **View in Lock Screen** setting to ON. When you receive new messages and your device is locked, you see a notification on the Locked screen. If the device is asleep, it wakes up and shows you the notification. If you take no action, the device goes back to sleep.

Changing iCloud-Specific Email Settings on an iOS Device

To do advanced configuration for only your iCloud account, perform the following steps:

1. Move into the Settings app if you aren't there already.

2. Tap **Mail, Contacts, Calendars**.

3. Tap your **iCloud account**.

4. Tap **Account**. You see the Account window that you use to change general aspects of your account, such as the storage plan you are using. These options are explained in Lesson 2.

5. Tap **Mail**. You see the Mail window. Here, you can configure your name, SMTP servers (where email is sent from) and if messages you delete are stored in the Archive folder. These options are also explained in Lesson 2.

6. Tap **Advanced**. You see the Advanced window.

7. Tap **Drafts Mailbox**. The Drafts Mailbox window has two sections. One is labeled On My *Device*, where *Device* is the name of the device you are using, and the other is labeled On the Server. The first section has only the Drafts option, while the second lists various folders on the iCloud server.

8. To store your draft messages only on your device, tap **Drafts** in the upper section; to store your draft messages on the server, tap one of the folders in the lower section (the Drafts folder on the server instead on your device). It's usually better to store drafts on a server folder because you can then get to them from any device. If you store them on your device, they are only available there.

9. Tap **Advanced**.

10. Tap **Sent Mailbox** and then tap a location to determine where your sent messages are stored. This works just like the setting that determines where your draft messages are stored.

11. Tap **Deleted Mailbox** to set the location for deleted messages. Typically, you are better off storing deleted messages on the device so messages you delete don't use your iCloud storage space.

12. Tap **Remove**.

13. Tap the amount of time you want to pass before messages you delete are removed from the Trash. It's generally a good idea to set this time relatively short, such as one day or one week so accumulated deleted messages don't use much of your iCloud storage space or device storage space (depending on the selection you made in step 11). (The S/MIME section, which you aren't likely to use, is explained in Lesson 2.)

You're done with the Advanced settings for your iCloud email account and are now ready to use the Mail app to work with your iCloud email.

NOTE: **More Info on the Mail App**

To learn how to use the Mail app, see my book *My iPhone, 5*[th] *Edition*, or *My iPod touch, 3*[rd] *Edition*.

Configuring iCloud Email on a Mac

Mail is Mac OS X's default email application. It is designed to seamlessly work with your iCloud email account. If you've already signed into your iCloud account on your Mac, you're ready to configure your iCloud email account in Mail. If not, go back to Lesson 3, "Configuring iCloud on Macintosh Computers," to complete that and then come back here.

First, ensure that your iCloud account is set to sync email by performing the following steps:

1. Open the System Preferences application.

2. Click the **iCloud** icon. The iCloud pane appears.

3. Ensure the **Mail & Notes** check box is checked, as shown in Figure 9.6. This ensures your email is synced on your Mac.

FIGURE 9.6   Check the Mail & Notes check box to sync your iCloud email on a Mac.

After you configure an iCloud account on a Mac, the next time you open the Mail application, the email account is configured for you automatically and is ready for you to use or to further configure as explained in the following steps:

1. Open the Mail application.

2. Choose **Mail**, **Preferences**.

3. Click the **Accounts** tab.

4. Select your **iCloud account** on the Accounts list in the left pane of the window. The account configuration tools appear in the right pane of the window.

5. Click the **Account Information** tab if it isn't selected already.

6. To change the description and "From" name for your account, edit the text in the **Description** and **Full Name** fields, respectively. The remaining fields are technical settings that enable you to receive and send email. You should not have to change any of these because they were configured for you automatically.

7. Click the **Mailbox Behaviors** tab.

8. Check the **Store draft message on the server** check box if you want any message drafts to be available on other devices.

9. To display notes in the Inbox in Mail, check the **Show notes in Inbox** check box. This is especially useful if you use the Notes

app on iOS devices because you have the same notes there and in Mail. (If you don't check this box, you can still work with your notes by selecting Notes on the Mailbox pane.)

10. Check the **Store sent messages on the server** check box to make your sent messages available to all your devices; leave this unchecked if you want messages you send to be stored on the Mac instead.

11. Use the **Sent** pop-up menu to determine when your sent messages are automatically deleted. The options include Never; when they are one week, one day, or one month old; or when you quit Mail.

12. Use the **Junk** check box and pop-up menu to determine how Mail deals with mail classified as junk; these work similarly to the Sent message tools.

13. Use the **Trash** tools to configure how Mail deals with messages you delete. As shown in Figure 9.7, there is an additional check box that determines if messages you delete are moved into the Trash folder.

14. Click the **Advanced** tab.

15. To temporarily disable the account, uncheck the **Enable this account** check box. This removes the iCloud mailboxes from Mail and stops checking for new messages. Check the check box to re-enable the iCloud email account.

16. If you want Mail to check for iCloud email when it checks for message automatically, check the **Include when automatically checking for new messages** check box.

17. If you want to be able to read messages and their attachments when you aren't connected to the Internet, choose **All messages and their attachments** on the Keep copies of messages for offline viewing pop-up menu. Other options include: don't keep any messages available, keep messages but not attachments, and keep only messages you've read. (There are several other settings on the Advanced tab, but you aren't likely to ever need to change them.)

18. Close the Accounts window and save your changes.

You can work with your iCloud email using all of Mail's great tools; this is a good thing because Mail offers lots of great features and functions. And because you can sync your iCloud email with your other devices, the same email messages are available to you no matter which device you happen to be using.

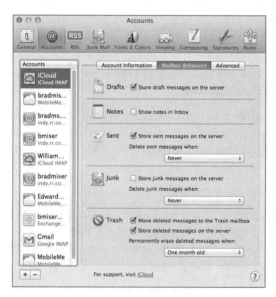

FIGURE 9.7   Use the Mailbox Behaviors tab to determine where Mail stores various kinds of emails and if notes are shown in your Inbox.

TIP: **Configuring iCloud Email Without Signing into iCloud**

If you use a Mac that isn't configured with your iCloud account, you can still use your iCloud email with it. Move to the Accounts pane and click the **Add (+)** button at the bottom of the Accounts list. Enter your full name, iCloud email address, and iCloud password. Then click **Create**. Check or uncheck the check boxes to enable or disable Calendar and Chat syncing. Then click **Create**. The iCloud email account is added to Mail, and you can work with it just like an account created for you.

Configuring iCloud Email on Windows PCs

Outlook is an extremely popular email client for Windows PCs. As you can probably guess, you can configure your iCloud email account in Outlook so you can use that application to work with your email. If Outlook is currently open, quit it before continuing in this section.

First, make sure email syncing is enabled by opening the iCloud control panel and checking the **Mail with Outlook** check box, as shown in Figure 9.8. Then, click **Apply**. (If you haven't set up iCloud on the PC yet, go back to Lesson 4, "Configuring iCloud on Windows Computers," and do so; then come back here.)

FIGURE 9.8   Check the Mail with Outlook check box to sync your iCloud email with Outlook on a Windows PC.

> NOTE: **Automatic Configuration**
>
> When you enable iCloud email on your computer, your account may be set up for you automatically. If it is, you will see it the next time you open Outlook. In that case, you will only have to enter your password to work with your iCloud email.

Second, add your iCloud account to Outlook by performing the following steps (which are for Outlook 2010; the steps for Outlook 2007 are similar):

1. Open the Outlook application.

2. Click the **File** tab.

3. Click **Info**.

4. Click **Add Account**. The Add New Account dialog appears.

5. Select the **E-mail Account** radio button.

6. Enter your name in the **Your Name** field.

7. Enter your iCloud email address in the **E-mail Address** field.

8. Enter your iCloud password in the **Password** and **Retype Password** fields.

9. When you've completed the fields, as shown in Figure 9.9, click **Next**. Outlook attempts to log into your account and then sends a test message. When the set up is complete, you see the configuration successful message.

10. Click **Finish**.

FIGURE 9.9   Adding an iCloud email account to Outlook is mostly a matter of completing this form.

After you set up your iCloud email account, you can work with it using Outlook's great email tools just like other accounts with which you use Outlook.

TIP: **Configuring iCloud Email in Other Email Applications**

Although it's designed for Mail on iOS devices and Macs and Outlook on Windows PCs, you can use your iCloud email account in any email application. You just need to manually configure your iCloud account in those applications. To get the detailed information you need to do this, visit http://support.apple.com/kb/HT4864.

Using the iCloud Mail Web Application

As if iOS devices, Macs, and Windows PCs weren't enough ways to use your iCloud email, you can also use the iCloud Mail web application. This application offers several of the same tools you find in a desktop application but has the benefit of being available on any computer running a supported web browser (Safari on a Mac or Safari or Internet Explorer on a Windows PC) and having an Internet connection.

To access the iCloud email web application, perform the following steps:

1. Log into your iCloud website (see Lesson 1, "Getting Started with Your iCloud Account and Website," for the details).

2. Click the **Application Switcher** button.

3. Click the **Mail** icon. You move into the web email application, as shown in Figure 9.10.

FIGURE 9.10   Using the iCloud Mail web application is a lot like using an email application on a computer.

If you've used an email application before, you won't have any trouble using the Mail web application. The following are some pointers for your consideration:

▶ The window has three panes, which are (from left to right): Mailboxes/Folders, Messages, and Reading. These work just like the panes in the Mail app on an iOS device or the Mail application on a Mac. Select the **mailbox** or **folder** containing the messages you want to see. The list of messages appears in the Messages pane. Select a **message** to view it in the Reading pane.

▶ You can resize the panes by dragging the vertical lines that separate them.

▶ To collapse or expand the Mailbox/Folder pane, click the **triangle inside a box** icon at the top of the message list pane.

▶ To check for new messages, click the **circled arrow** just to the right of Mailboxes in the upper-left corner of the window.

▶ You can create new folders on the server by clicking the **Add (+)** button at the top of the Folders section. Name the folder and press **Return** (Mac) or **Enter** (Windows) to save it.

▶ You can move messages to a folder by dragging them from a mailbox into a folder. Any folders you create are available on any device accessing your account.

▶ You can sort messages in the Messages pane using the pop-up menu at the top. Options include: Date, From, Subject, and so on. You can also choose the sort order.

▶ Click the **Action (gear)** button to access a number of useful commands. Preferences enables you to set a number of preferences that determine how the application works; these include viewing, forwarding, where messages are saved, default settings for new messages, email rules, and the "vacation" settings to create an automatic reply to mail you receive. Other commands include Mark, which you can use to mark messages; Delete Folder, to remove folders you no longer need; Empty Trash, to permanently remove deleted messages; and Print, to print email messages.

Working with Email Aliases

One of the benefits of iCloud email is that you can have up to three email aliases. An alias is an email address that you can create that points to your iCloud account but hides your actual iCloud account/Apple ID. These are really useful for shielding your primary address, such as to protect it from spam or to have an address for a specific purpose. For example, an iCloud account name might be something like sirwilliamwallace@me.com. If this were my account and I wanted to promote a book I was writing, I could create an alias such as styicloud@me.com. When people send email to that address it comes to the same place, though it appears to be a different address.

Aliases are really good to use in places where you are likely to get spammed, such as online shopping, forums, and so on. If an alias gets spammed, you can simply delete it, and your spam troubles are gone. You can create a replacement for it quite easily.

To create an alias, perform the following steps:

1. Open the Mail web application.

2. Click the **Action** (gear) button.

3. Choose **Preferences**.

4. Click the **Addresses** tab.

5. Click **Add an alias**. The Create Mail Alias sheet appears.

6. Create the alias by typing in the **Alias** field.

7. Enter the name you want to appear as the From address in the **Full Name** field. This can be any name you want; it doesn't have to be your real name and shouldn't be if you are creating the address for protection against spam.

8. Enter a description of the alias in the **Description** field. This can be helpful to remember why you created the alias later on.

9. Click the **Label Color** to associate with the alias. When you receive messages, they are coded with the color you select, making it easier to know when the mail was sent to an alias as opposed to your actual iCloud address.

10. When you're ready to create the alias, as shown in Figure 9.11, click **OK**. The alias is checked to make sure no one else is using it and it doesn't violate any rules. If either of these is true, you have to change the alias until they aren't. When the alias passes inspection, you see the Mail Alias Created sheet.

11. Click **Done**. The alias is ready to use.

FIGURE 9.11   An alias is useful for shielding your iCloud address or for special purposes, such as promoting a book.

When someone sends email to an alias, it comes into your mailbox just like email sent to your iCloud email address. The To address is the alias, and it is color-coded as indicated. You can send email from an alias too, which is especially important in the fight against spam.

> TIP: **Aliases in Mac OS X Mail**
>
> To administer your aliases in Mac OS X's Mail application, open its Preferences dialog, click the **Accounts** tab, click **Account Information**, and then click **Edit Email Aliases**. This takes you to the Addresses tab of the Preferences window in the Mail web application.

You can use the Addresses tab of the preferences window to also do the following:

▶ To delete an alias you no longer want, select it and click **Delete Alias**.

▶ You can also change an alias' description, name, and associated color.

▶ To temporarily disable an alias, uncheck the **Receive mail and send mail** from the alias check box.

> NOTE: **MobileMe and Email Aliases**
>
> The previous iteration of iCloud was MobileMe. Although iCloud is much better than MobileMe in many ways, MobileMe was slightly better in the alias department. The good news is that you can continue to use aliases created under MobileMe. The bad news is that under MobileMe, you could have up to five email aliases. If you have four or five aliases, you have to delete two or three respectively to be able to create a new one because iCloud only supports three per account.

Summary

In this lesson, you learned how to use your iCloud email account on iOS devices and computers, as well as how to use the iCloud email web application. In the next lesson, you learn how to use iCloud for your contacts.

LESSON 10

Using iCloud to Manage Your Contacts

In this lesson, you learn how to use iCloud to manage your contact information on iOS devices and computers.

Using iCloud to Manage Contact Information

Using a contact manager application is a great way to keep track of the information you need to keep in touch with people by phone, email, chat, texting, tweeting, and well, you get the idea. It's likely that you use contact information on several devices. For example, you might make phone calls and send text messages on an iPhone or email and chat using a computer.

iCloud is extremely useful in helping you keep your contact information current and available everywhere you need it, including on iOS devices, Macintosh computers, and Windows computers. After you've enabled contact syncing via iCloud, you have the same contact information available to you on each device; any changes you make on one device are automatically made on the other devices too.

iCloud contact syncing is designed to work with the following:

▶ The Contacts app on iOS devices

▶ Address Book on Macintosh computers

▶ Outlook on Windows computers

▶ The iCloud Contacts web application

Configuring iCloud for Contacts on an iOS Device

To ensure contact information is communicated to and from the cloud, you need to configure each iOS device to include contact information in the sync process. You can also change the settings that impact how contact information is displayed on your iOS devices.

Configuring iCloud Contact Syncing on an iOS Device

To include contact information on an iOS device in the sync process, perform the following steps:

1. Open the Settings app.

2. Tap **iCloud**.

3. Set the **Contacts** switch to ON, as shown in Figure 10.1. Contact information on the device is copied to and from the cloud.

FIGURE 10.1   Setting Contacts to ON causes an iOS device to sync contact information with the cloud.

Configuring How Contacts Display on an iOS Device

On an iOS device, you can configure some aspects of how contact information is displayed in the Contacts app and wherever contact information is displayed (such as when you look up a phone number on an iPhone). You can determine how contacts are sorted on lists by first or last name, and you can choose which of those appears first on lists. Configure your contact preferences by following these steps:

1. Open the Settings app.

2. Tap **Mail, Contacts, Calendars**.

3. Scroll down until you see the Contacts section, as shown in Figure 10.2.

FIGURE 10.2   Use the Contacts section to configure your contact preferences.

4. Tap **Sort Order**.

5. To have contacts sorted by first name and then last name, tap **First, Last**.

6. To have contacts sorted by last name and then first name, tap **Last, First**.

7. Tap the **Back** button, which is labeled **Mail** on an iPhone or iPod touch or **Mail, Contacts** on an iPad.

8. Tap **Display Order**.

9. To show contacts in the format first name, last name, tap **First, Last**.

10. To show contacts in the format last name, first name, tap **Last, First**.

11. Tap the **Back** button, which is labeled **Mail** on an iPhone or iPod touch or **Mail, Contacts** on an iPad.

12. Tap **My Info**.

13. Use the Contacts app to find and tap your contact information. This tells the device your contact information, which it can insert for you in various places. You return to the Mail, Contacts, Calendars screen and see the contact information you selected next to My Info.

14. If you have more than one account for which contact syncing is enabled, tap **Default Account**.

15. Tap the account you want to be the default for contact information.

16. Tap the **Back** button, which is labeled **Mail** on an iPhone or iPod touch or **Mail, Contacts** on an iPad.

Configuring iCloud Contact Syncing on a Mac

You can sync contact information on a Mac by performing the following steps:

1. Open the System Preferences application.

2. Click the **iCloud** icon. The iCloud pane opens, as shown in Figure 10.3.

3. Check the **Contacts** check box.

FIGURE 10.3   When you enable contact syncing on a Mac, your contact information in Address Book is stored in the cloud.

After you've enabled contact syncing, contact information in the Address Book application is uploaded to the cloud, from where it is synced to other devices. Any changes you make on any device are communicated from the device to the cloud and back to your other devices.

NOTE: **Contacts from Other Accounts**

A number of services can store your contact information and can be synced on your devices, the most significant of which is Exchange. When syncing is enabled for these accounts, within the contacts application, such as Address Book on a Mac or the Contacts app on iOS devices, you can select specific accounts to work with the contact information stored there.

Configuring iCloud Contact Syncing on a Windows PC

On a Windows PC, you can enable contact syncing with Outlook by configuring the iCloud control panel as described in the following steps:

1. Open the iCloud control panel.

2. Check the **Contacts with Outlook** check box, as shown in Figure 10.4.

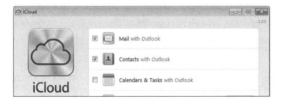

FIGURE 10.4   You can sync contact information in Outlook via your iCloud account.

3. Click **Apply**. If Outlook is open, you're prompted to close it so your contacts can be added to it.

4. When you see the Setup is complete dialog box, click **Done**.

After you've enabled contact syncing, your iCloud contacts are available in the Outlook application, as shown in Figure 10.5.

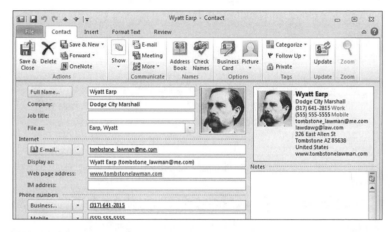

FIGURE 10.5   Here, you see contact information from the cloud being displayed in Outlook.

Using the iCloud Contacts Web Application

On your iCloud website, you can use the Contacts web application to access your contact information from any computer that runs a supported web browser and has an Internet connection. This is convenient for those likely but rare times when you don't have one of your other devices available to you.

To access the iCloud Contacts web application, perform the following steps:

1. Log into your iCloud website (see Lesson 1, "Getting Started with Your iCloud Account and Website," for the details).

2. Click the **Application Switcher** button.

3. Click the **Contacts** icon. You move into the web contacts application, as shown in Figure 10.6.

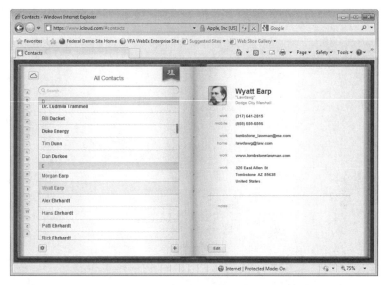

FIGURE 10.6   The Contacts app on your iCloud website simulates an address book.

> **NOTE: iCloud Contacts App Seem Familiar?**
>
> If you use Address Book on a Mac or the Contacts app on an iOS device, the web application will look familiar to you because it provides a very similar interface.

Following are some pointers about using the Contacts web application:

► The contacts available to you are on the left-hand page when you see the icon with two silhouettes at the top just to the left of the center of the "book." The name of the page is the name of the contact group with which you are working.

► When you click the **icon with two silhouettes**, the list of contacts moves to the right-hand page. On the left-hand page, you see your contact groups. When you select a **group**, you see a list of the contacts it contains on the right-hand page and will be working with that group as shown in Figure 10.7. To work with all your contacts, select **All Contacts**.

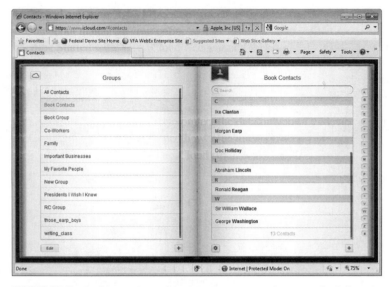

FIGURE 10.7 In this mode, your contact groups are shown on the left and the contacts in the selected group are on the right.

▶ To create a new group, click the **Add (+)** button near the center of the page at the bottom. A new group is created. Name it and press **Return** (Mac) or **Enter** (Windows).

▶ You can then place contacts in groups by dragging them from the right-hand page and dropping them onto the group in which you want them to be stored on the left-hand page. Contacts can be stored in more than one group at the same time.

▶ Click the **icon with one silhouette**; the list of contacts in the group you selected is shown on the left-hand page. You can browse the list or search it by entering search information in the Search bar at the top of the window. You can click letters on the "index" along the left edge of the "book" to jump to a specific section of contacts.

▶ When you select a **contact** on the left-hand page, you see detailed information for that contact on the right-hand page.

▶ To change a contact's information, click the **Edit** button. The contact page moves into edit mode, and you can change its information. Click **Done** when you've made all the changes you want to make.

▶ To add a new contact, click the **Add (+)** button located near the middle of the screen at the bottom. Complete the resulting form to create the contact.

▶ Click the **Action (gear)** button to see a menu of additional commands.

▶ If you choose the **Preferences** command on that menu, you can set display and format options for your contacts in the web application.

▶ Choose **Make This My Card** to select your own contact information, which is used in the other applications. This also becomes your contact information on your other devices.

▶ Choose **Refresh Contacts** to manually sync the web application with your other contact applications running on various devices.

Summary

In this lesson, you learned how to use iCloud to help you manage your contact information on iOS devices and computers and how to use the Contacts web application. In the next lesson, you learn how to do the same for your calendars.

LESSON 11

Using iCloud with Your Calendars

In this lesson, you learn how to use iCloud to manage your calendars on iOS devices and computers and how to use the iCloud Calendar web application.

Using iCloud to Manage Your Calendars

A calendar application is a great way to keep track of important, and even not so important, events in your life. Using a calendar application on a computer is useful, but having your calendars with you at all times on your iOS devices is even better because you can manage your life while you are on the move.

iCloud helps you keep your calendars current and available everywhere you need them, including on iOS devices, Macintosh computers, and Windows computers. After you've enabled calendar syncing via iCloud, you have the same calendars available to you on each device; any changes, such as creating a new event, you make on one device are automatically available on the other devices too. You can also use the iCloud Calendar web application to access your calendars from any computer with a supported web browser and an Internet connection.

iCloud calendar syncing is designed to work with the following:

- ▶ The Calendar app on iOS devices
- ▶ iCal on Macintosh computers
- ▶ Outlook on Windows computers
- ▶ The iCloud Calendar web application

Configuring iCloud Calendars on an iOS Device

To ensure your calendar information is communicated to and from the cloud, you need to configure each iOS device to include calendar information in the sync process. You can also change your calendar preferences on your iOS devices.

Configuring iCloud Calendar Syncing on an iOS Device

To include calendar information on an iOS device in the sync process, perform the following steps:

1. Open the Settings app.

2. Tap **iCloud**.

3. Set the **Calendars** switch to ON, as shown in Figure 11.1. Calendar information on the device is copied to and from the cloud.

FIGURE 11.1   Setting Calendars to ON causes an iOS device to sync your calendars with the cloud.

Configuring Calendar Preferences on an iOS Device

You can change a number of aspects of how calendars work on your iOS devices. Before jumping into the steps, however, one of the Calendar app's functions requires a bit of explanation.

The Time Zone Support feature associates time zones with your events. This can be a useful thing, but it also can be a bit confusing. If Time Zone Support is enabled (ON), the iOS device displays event times according to the time zone associated with the time zone selected on the Time Zone Support screen. (You learn about this shortly.) When Time Zone Support is disabled (OFF), the time zone used for calendars is the device's current time zone that is set automatically based on your network connection or your manual setting; this means that when you change time zones (automatically or manually), the times for calendar events shift accordingly.

For example, suppose you set Indianapolis (which is in the Eastern time zone) as the device's time zone. If you enable Time Zone Support and then set San Francisco as the time zone for Time Zone Support. The events on your calendars are shown according to the Pacific time zone because that is San Francisco's time zone rather than Eastern time (Indianapolis' time zone).

In other words, when Time Zone Support is ON, the dates and times for events become fixed based on the time zone you select for Time Zone Support. If you change the time zone the device is in, there is no change to the dates and times for events shown on the calendar because they remain set according to the Time Zone Support time zone you select.

In any case, you need to be aware of the time zone you are using for your calendars (the one you select if Time Zone Support is ON or the time zone of your current location if it is OFF) and the time zone with which events are associated.

> NOTE: **Time Zone Support in Calendar Applications**
>
> With some calendar applications (such as iCal on a Mac), you can associate an event with a specific time zone when you schedule it. This is useful because events shift with the device's time zone; for example, if you schedule a meeting for 3 PM in the Eastern time zone and then travel to the Pacific time zone, the meeting moves on the calendar to reflect a 12 PM start time.

Configure your calendar preferences by following these steps:

1. Open the Settings app.

2. Tap **Mail, Contacts, Calendars**.

3. Scroll down until you see the Calendars section, as shown in Figure 11.2.

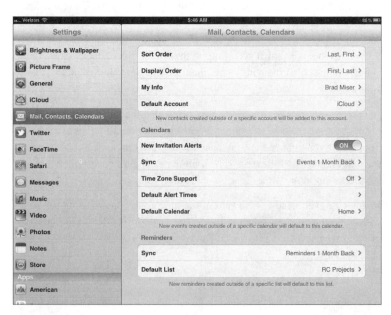

FIGURE 11.2   Use the tools in the Calendars section to configure your calendar preferences.

4. If you don't want to be alerted when you receive invitations to events, set the **New Invitation Alerts** switch to OFF. When you are invited to events, you won't see notifications. To be alerted again, tap OFF to toggle the status back ON.

5. To set the period of time over which past events are synced, tap **Sync**.

6. Tap the amount of time you want events to be synced; tap **All Events** to have all events synced, regardless of their age. For example, if you tap **Event 1 Month Back**, your calendars in the Calendar app show events within the past month.

7. Tap the Back button, which is labeled **Mail** on an iPhone or iPod touch or **Mail, Contacts** on an iPad.

8. Tap **Time Zone Support**.

9. To have the device display meeting and event times on its calendars based on the device's current time zone (either set automatically through the cellular network or set manually), set the **Time Zone Support** switch to OFF and skip to step 14.

10. To have event times displayed according to a specific time zone, set the **Time Zone Support** switch to ON and move to the next step.

11. Tap **Time Zone**.

12. Type the name of the city you want to use to set the time zone. As you type, the Settings app lists the cities that match your search.

13. When the city you want to use appears on the list, tap it. You move back to the Time Zone Support screen, and the city you selected is shown in the Time Zone field.

14. Tap the Back button, which is labeled **Mail** on an iPhone or iPod touch or **Mail, Contacts** on an iPad.

15. Tap **Default Alert Times**.

16. Tap the item for which you want to set a default alert time; the options are **Birthdays**, **Events**, and **All-Day Events**, as shown in Figure 11.3.

FIGURE 11.3 You can choose the default alert times for items on your calendars using this screen.

17. Tap the alert time that you want to set as the default for the type of item you tapped in step 16. For example, if you tap **Events** and then tap **30 minutes before**, when you create a new event on your device, it will have a 30-minute alert set automatically. You can change the alerts for any event so this setting just gives you a starting point.

18. Tap **Default Alert Times**.

19. Set the default alert times for the other two items using steps 16 through 18.

20. Tap the Back button, which is labeled **Mail** on an iPhone or iPod touch or **Mail, Contacts** on an iPad.

21. Tap **Default Calendar** (if you have only one calendar on your device, skip this and the next step). You see the list of all calendars configured on the iOS device based on its sync settings.

22. Tap the calendar that you want to be the default, meaning the one that is selected unless you specifically choose a different one. When you create a new event, you can change the calendar on which it appears; this setting only determines the initial calendar for new events.

Configuring iCloud Calendar Syncing on a Mac

You can sync calendar information on a Mac by following these steps:

1. Open the System Preferences application.

2. Click the **iCloud** icon. The iCloud pane opens, as shown in Figure 11.4.

3. Check the **Calendars** check box.

FIGURE 11.4   When you enable calendar syncing on a Mac, your calendar information in iCloud is stored in the cloud.

After you enabled calendar syncing, iCloud calendar information in the iCal application, as shown in Figure 11.5, is uploaded to the cloud, from where it is synced to other devices. Any changes you make on any device are communicated to the cloud and back to your other devices.

NOTE: **Calendars from Other Accounts**

A number of services can store your calendars and can be synced on your devices, with one of the most useful being Exchange. Within the calendar application, such as iCal on a Mac or the Calendar app on iOS devices, you can select specific accounts to work with the calendar information stored there.

FIGURE 11.5   You can use iCal on a Mac to display and manage your iCloud calendars.

Configuring iCloud Calendar Syncing on a Windows PC

On a Windows PC, you can enable calendar syncing with Outlook by configuring the iCloud control panel as described in the following steps:

1. Open the iCloud control panel.

2. Check the **Calendars & Tasks with Outlook** check box, as shown in Figure 11.6.

3. Click **Apply**. If Outlook is open, you're prompted to close it so your calendar information can be added to it.

4. When you see the Setup is complete dialog box, click **Done**.

After you enable calendar syncing, your iCloud calendars are available in Outlook, as shown in Figure 11.7.

FIGURE 11.6   You can sync calendar information in Outlook via your iCloud account.

FIGURE 11.7   Here, you see calendar information from the cloud displayed in Outlook.

Using the iCloud Calendar Web Application

On your iCloud website, you can use the Calendar web application to access your calendar information from any computer that runs a supported web browser and has an Internet connection. This is convenient when you don't have one of your other devices available to you.

To access the iCloud Calendar web application, perform the following steps:

1. Log into your iCloud website (see Lesson 1, "Getting Started with Your iCloud Account and Website," for the details).

2. Click the **Application Switcher** button.

3. Click the **Calendar** icon. You move into the web calendar application, as shown in Figure 11.8.

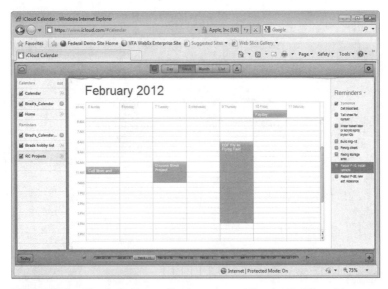

FIGURE 11.8 The Calendar application on your iCloud website enables you to manage your calendars from just about any computer.

Following are some pointers about using the Calendar web application:

▶ The calendars available to you are shown on the Calendars list on the far left pane of the window. You can show or hide the list of calendars by clicking the button just to the left of the Day button. Hiding it provides more room in the window for calendars.

▶ To show a specific calendar, check its check box. When you uncheck a calendar's check box, its events are hidden but unchanged. You can display them again by checking the calendar's check box.

▶ You can change how the calendar is displayed by clicking any of the following: **Day**, **Week**, **Month**, or **List**. The window changes to reflect your selection. The Day option presents calendars in a "calendar book" with each day shown on two pages; the left-hand page shows detail for the day's events while the right-hand page shows an overview of the day. **Week** shows a full week of days, and you can probably guess what clicking the **Month** button shows. The List option includes two panes; the left pane shows a month at a glance view, and the right pane shows detail for the selected day.

▶ Change the timeframe shown on the calendar using the scroll bar and arrows at the bottom of the window. This shows the context of the view currently selected; for example, when the **Week** view is selected, you see buttons that represent weeks.

▶ To create an event, click the **Add (+)** button located in the bottom right corner of the window. Use the resulting dialog box to record the event's details, including name, location, and other details. Click **OK** to create the event on the selected calendar.

▶ Open the Action menu by clicking the **gear** button in the upper right corner of the window. You see a number of useful commands, including Preferences, various new commands, Delete Event, Go to commands, Hide and Show commands, and Refresh Calendar (which causes your calendars to be updated).

> NOTE: **Reminders**
>
> Reminders are notifications you can set to remind you of just about anything. You can manage your reminders in the Reminders app on iOS devices or in iCal and Outlook (reminders are called tasks in Outlook). The far right pane in the Calendar application shows your reminders. You learn more about reminders in Lesson 12, "Using iCloud to Sync Other Information."

Summary

In this lesson, you learned how to use iCloud to help you manage your calendar on iOS devices and computers and how to use the Calendar web application. In the next lesson, you learn how to use iCloud to sync other kinds of information, such as your bookmarks.

LESSON 12

Using iCloud to Sync Other Information

In this lesson, you learn how to include bookmarks, notes, and reminders in your syncs so you can share these items on all your devices.

Understanding Other Sync Options

In the previous lessons, you learned about the "more important" sync options, which include email, calendars, and contacts. In this lesson, you learn about other sync options that are also useful. These include the following:

▶ **Reminders (called tasks in Outlook).** Reminders (tasks) can be just about anything you want to be reminded about. You can enter the text for a reminder and then configure how, where, and when you want to be reminded about the "thing." Of course reminders can be for tasks that you need to do and are just as useful, if not more useful, for general information, such as something you want to remember. On iOS devices, you use the Reminders app; on Macs, manage reminders in iCal; and on Windows PCs, manage reminders (tasks) in Outlook.

▶ **Bookmarks.** You can use this feature to ensure you have the same set of bookmarks in your web browser on any device. On iOS devices and Macs, synced bookmarks are available in Safari, and on a Windows PC they are available in Internet Explorer or Safari.

▶ **Notes.** These are text "snippets" that can capture any text you want. To work with notes on an iOS device, you use the Notes app. On a Mac, notes appear in Mail. On a Windows PC, you currently can't sync notes via iCloud (another way to sync is explained later in this lesson).

Configuring Other Sync Options on an iOS Device

To configure any of the previously mentioned sync options on an iOS device, perform the following steps:

1. Open the Settings app.

2. Tap **iCloud**. The iCloud settings screen opens, as shown in Figure 12.1.

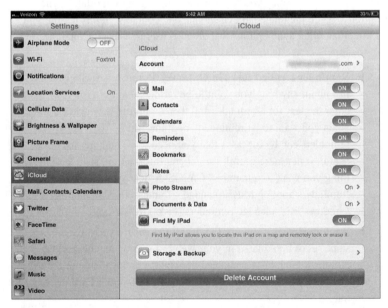

FIGURE 12.1   You can also include reminders, bookmarks, and notes in your iCloud syncs on iOS devices.

3. To include reminders in your syncs, set the **Reminders** switch to ON.

4. To include your Safari bookmarks in your syncs, set the **Bookmarks** switch to ON.

5. To do the same for your notes, set the **Notes** switch to ON.

After you've enabled these options, work with them in the following apps:

▶ Use the Reminders app to view, create, and manage your reminders. You can include a number of elements in your reminders, such as notes, priorities, and so on, as shown in Figure 12.2. On an iPhone, you can even trigger reminders based on your location, such as when you arrive or leave a specific location.

FIGURE 12.2   Reminders on an iPhone can be triggered by location changes.

▶ You can use your bookmarks in the Safari app.

▶ To work with notes, use the Notes app. You can create multiple notes; you can copy and paste content to and from the Notes app in addition to typing it in. On an iPhone 4S, you can use Siri to dictate notes.

Configuring Other Sync Options on a Mac

To set up these sync options on a Mac, do the following:

1. Open the iCloud pane of the System Preferences, as shown in Figure 12.3.

2. To sync your notes, ensure the **Mail & Notes** check box is checked.

FIGURE 12.3   Use the iCloud pane of the System Preferences application to configure your additional sync options on a Mac.

NOTE: **No Separate Syncs**

On a Mac, you can only sync notes and reminders if you sync email and calendar information. That's because notes are managed in the Mail email application, and reminders are managed in iCal.

3. To sync your reminders, check the **Calendars** check box.

4. To sync your bookmarks, check the **Bookmarks** check box.

To work with your synced information, use the following applications:

▶ Use Mail to work with your notes. Confusingly, notes appear in the *REMINDERS* section on the Mailbox list. Working with your notes is similar to working with email messages, in that you can select a note on the notes list and it appears in the reading pane.

> TIP: **Notes in Your Inbox**
>
> If you prefer, you can access notes directly in your Inbox. Open the Mail Preferences dialog box, click the **Accounts** tab, select your iCloud account, click the **Mailbox Behaviors** sub-tab, and check the **Show notes in Inbox** check box.

▶ You can use iCal to work with reminders. Reminders appear in the Reminders pane, which you can show or hide with a command on the View menu. Reminders in iCal can contain similar information to reminders in the Reminders app on an iOS device, though you can't trigger reminders by location changes.

▶ Your synced bookmarks are available in the Safari web browser.

Configuring Other Sync Options on a Windows PC

To configure these sync options on a Windows PC, perform the following steps:

1. Open the iCloud control panel, as shown in Figure 12.4.

2. To sync your reminders, check the **Calendars & Tasks with Outlook** check box.

3. To sync your bookmarks, check the **Bookmarks with *browser*** check box, where *browser* is the currently selected web browser.

4. Click the **Options** button.

FIGURE 12.4   Use the iCloud control panel to configure your additional sync options on a Windows PC.

5. Select the web browser in which you want to use your synced bookmarks. The options are Internet Explorer or Safari. (You only see the Options button if Safari is installed on your computer.)

6. Click **OK**.

7. Click **Apply**.

To access these items, use the following applications:

▶ In Outlook, reminders are called tasks. Open Outlook and click the Tasks option. In the iCloud section, you see the reminders that have been synced via iCloud. You can open and edit the tasks (reminders) you see, as shown in Figure 12.5. To create a new task on iCloud, select the reminder list on which you want the reminder created and click New Task. (The first time you create a task, you must supply your iCloud password.)

▶ To use your synced bookmarks, use the web browser you selected in step 5.

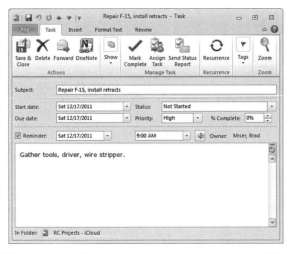

FIGURE 12.5   Use the iCloud control panel to configure your additional sync options on a Windows PC.

TIP: **Syncing Notes on a Windows PC**

On a Windows PC, you can't currently use iCloud to sync notes. You can sync notes with iOS devices using iTunes. Connect the device to your computer and select it on the iTunes Source list. Click the Info tab. Check the Sync notes with check box and choose the application with which you want them synced on the drop-down list. When you sync the device, your notes move to and from the application you selected. When your notes are on the iOS device, they get synced via iCloud to other devices. However, you have to manually sync a device to get your notes on a Windows PC.

Summary

In this lesson, you learned how to include bookmarks, notes, and reminders in your syncs. In the next lesson, you learn how to use iCloud to safeguard your devices and data.

LESSON 13

Using iCloud to Locate and Secure Your Devices

In this lesson, you learn how to use iCloud to locate missing devices and to protect their data.

Using iCloud to Find Devices

iOS devices are mobile; they can easily go anywhere because they are small and lightweight. They are also powerful and can store all kinds of sensitive data, from contacts to personal information you use for financial activity and other sensitive content. These two factors make the devices extremely useful. However, this also means that if you lose control of a device, bad things can happen. At worst, someone could compromise your data to steal your identity or take money from you.

Laptop computers present a similar risk. Although not quite as mobile as an iOS device, laptops can also become separated from their owners in a number of ways, from simply being misplaced to getting stolen.

iCloud includes the Find My *Device* application, where *Device* can be an iPad, iPod, iPhone, or Mac. This feature enables you to locate a device remotely. When located, you can lock the device, or if you feel you have lost control of it, you can erase its memory.

To use this feature, you must first enable it on each device. After it's enabled, you can locate and secure devices through your iCloud website.

NOTE: **No Find My PC**

You might have noticed that I did not mention a Windows PC on the list of devices that you can find via iCloud. This feature only supports Apple devices; Windows PCs are not supported. So you'll need to find some other way to accomplish these tasks for your Windows PCs. There are many options a web search can reveal to you.

Finding iOS Devices

Finding iOS devices via iCloud requires that you set up each device to use this feature. When that is done, you can use the Find My *Device* application on your iCloud website to locate a device, and then you can perform several different actions to secure it.

Enabling Find My iPhone on iOS Devices

To enable an iOS to be found, perform the following steps:

1. On the Settings screen, tap **iCloud**.

2. If OFF is displayed next to Find My *Device*, where *Device* is iPad, iPhone, or iPod, tap the **switch** to set it in the ON position; if ON is displayed, skip the rest of these steps.

3. Tap **Allow** at the prompt.

4. If prompted, enable **Location Services**. The Find My *Device* feature becomes active, as shown in Figure 13.1, and iCloud starts tracking the location of the device.

NOTE: **Location Services**

Find My *Device* works through the Location Services feature of iOS devices. A device can be located based upon its Internet connection via a Wi-Fi or cellular Internet connection or via GPS. GPS location is most accurate, but iPhones and iPads with 3G support are the only iOS devices that offer it.

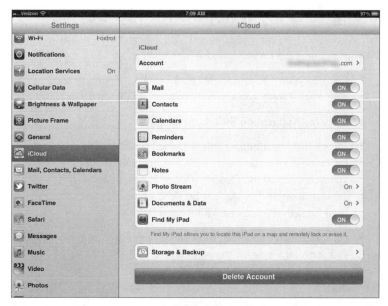

FIGURE 13.1 With Find My iPad enabled, this device can be tracked via the iCloud website.

NOTE: **Passcode**

A passcode is a four-digit number (simple) or longer string of characters (complex) that must be entered to unlock an iOS device. You should configure and use a passcode on your devices if there is any chance they can get out of your control. Without entering the correct passcode, the device can't be unlocked, and so it can't be used, thus your data is protected. To configure a passcode, open the Settings app. Tap **General** and then tap **Passcode Lock**. From there, you can choose the type of passcode you want and configure it. When you've done that, the passcode is required each time you unlock the device.

Using Find My iPhone with iOS Devices

When activated, you can access your device's location via your iCloud website by doing the following tasks:

1. Log into your iCloud website (see Lesson 1, "Getting Started with Your iCloud Account and Website" for the details).

2. Click the **Application Switcher** button.

3. Click **Find My iPhone**. (This is labeled Find My iPhone no matter which device you are locating.) All the iOS devices for which you have enabled the Find My *Device* feature under your iCloud are shown on the My Devices list. If a device is online and has been located, it is marked with a green dot.

4. Click the **device** you want to locate. If the device can be located, you see it on a map, as shown in Figure 13.2.

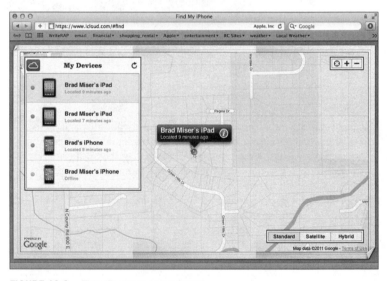

FIGURE 13.2   This iPad has been found.

5. Click the device's **Info (i)** button. You see the Info dialog, as shown in Figure 13.3. This dialog enables you to take several

actions on the device, which are explained in the following
paragraphs.

FIGURE 13.3   This dialog enables you to perform an action on a device
you've found.

When you have located a device, you can perform the following actions:

▶ **Play a sound or send a message.** This does just what it sounds
   like. A sound, message, or both is played on the device. This provides information to whomever has the device—such as if you've
   loaned the device to someone and want it back. The sound can
   help you locate the device if it is in the same general vicinity you
   are in.

▶ **Remote lock.** This locks the device so it can't be used. This can
   protect your device without changing its data.

▶ **Remote wipe.** This erases the device's memory as the "last
   chance" to protect your data. You should only do this in the
   worst-case scenario.

Each of these actions is explained in the following steps.

To send a sound or message to an iOS device:

1. Locate the device and open the Info dialog box.

2. Click **Play Sound or Send Message**.

3. Type the message you want to display.

4. If you want a sound to play, set the Sound status to ON, as shown in Figure 13.4.

FIGURE 13.4   A message is entered and a sound is set to play.

NOTE: **The Sound Remains the Same**

When you send a sound to a device you are finding, it plays even if the device is muted.

---

5. Click **Send**. The message is sent to the device, as shown in Figure 13.5, and the sound is played if you enabled that option. You also receive a confirmation email to the email address associated with your Apple ID that displays the message.

FIGURE 13.5   On the iPad, the message has been received, and a sound is playing.

To stop the sound from playing on the device, unlock it and tap the OK button on the message prompt. (If you don't require a passcode, anyone who has the phone can do this, which is one reason requiring a passcode is more secure.)

To prevent someone from using a device, you can lock it remotely by doing the following:

1. Locate the device and open the Info dialog box.

2. Click **Remote Lock**. What happens next depends on if the device has a passcode or not.

3. If the device currently has a passcode, skip to step 7.

4. If you haven't entered a passcode on the device (which you should have per the earlier sidebar), you're prompted to create a password by entering it.

5. Re-enter it at the prompt.

6. Click **Lock** and skip the next step.

7. Click **Lock** *Device* where *Device* is the name of the device you want to lock.

When you perform step 6 or 7, the Lock command is sent to the device, and the Info dialog for the device shows that it is locked. Either the passcode you created or the device's existing password must be entered for the device to be unlocked and used.

NOTE: **Auto-Lock**

The Auto-Lock feature causes an iOS device to automatically lock after a specific period of inactive time has passed. If you protect your iOS device with a passcode, you should also set the Auto-Lock. After the inactive time passes, the device locks, and the passcode is required to unlock it. This minimizes the time during which the device is vulnerable if you lose control of it. To set the Auto-Lock, open the Settings app. Tap **General** and then tap **Auto-Lock**.

If you decide you've lost control of your device, take the following steps:

1. Locate the device and open the Info dialog box.

2. Click **Remote Wipe**.

CAUTION: **Wiping a Device**

When you wipe a device, all its data is deleted, and it is reset to factory conditions. This means you will no longer be able to use Find My iPhone to locate it. Only do this when you're pretty sure the device is out of your control or that you won't be getting it back any time soon.

---

3. Click **Wipe** *Device*, where *Device* is the name of the device, as shown in Figure 13.6. All the data on your device is erased, and it is restored to factory settings.

FIGURE 13.6   When all hope of a quick recovery is lost, wipe a device to protect its data.

Here are a few more tidbits to facilitate finding your devices:

▶ To update the location of your device, click the **Refresh (curved arrow)** button in the upper right corner of the My Devices list.

▶ If you lose control of your device, use an escalation of steps to try to regain control. Immediately play a sound and send a message to it and then lock it. This will hopefully prevent someone else from using it while you locate it. If the device is near you and you've just forgotten where it is, the sound might help you find it again. If you don't get results, you can wipe the device to delete the data it contains. This is a severe action, so you don't want to do it prematurely.

> TIP: **What Message to Send?**
>
> When you send a message to a device, include your contact information in the message, such as a phone number where you can be reached. You could also offer a reward for the return of the device if you wanted to. Include enough information so if someone wants to return the device to you, they will be able to do so.

▶ Remote wiping is a bit of a two-edged sword. It protects your data by erasing your device, which also means you can't use Find My iPhone to locate it anymore. You should only use this if you're pretty sure that someone has your device because after you wipe it, there's no way to try to track the device's location. How fast you move to a wipe also depends on if you've required a passcode. If you do require a passcode, you know that your device's data can't be accessed without that code, so it will take some time for a miscreant to crack it, and you might be slower on the Erase All Data trigger. If your device doesn't have a passcode, you might want to pull the trigger faster. If you do recover your phone after a wipe, go through the restore process to return your device to its condition as of your most recent backup.

▶ As you use Find My iPhone, you receive email notifications about various events, such as when a device is locked, when a message you sent is displayed, and so on. These are a good way to know something about what is happening with your device even though you might not be able to see the device for yourself.

▶ If Find My iPhone can't find a device, select it on the list of devices. The device is shown in the right part of the window. You can initiate the same actions as when the device is found, though they won't actually happen until the device becomes visible again. To be notified when this happens, check the **Email me when this *device* is found** check box. When the device becomes visible to Find My iPhone, you receive an email and then can take appropriate action to locate and secure it.

▶ The circle around a device's dot indicates how precise its location is. The larger the circle, the less precise the device's location.

▶ There's an app for that. You can download and use the free Find My iPhone app on an iOS device to use this feature. For example, you can use this app on an iPhone to locate an iPad.

CAUTION: **No Security Is Perfect**

Even with passcodes, Auto-Lock, and the Find My iPhone, your information stored on an iOS device can be compromised. For example, if you don't have a passcode, someone can easily disable the device's network connections, thus eliminating your ability to find it. While disconnected, someone can access the device's data. However, these features require that someone trying to gain access to your information be much more sophisticated to be able to do so (than if you do not use these features). This will be beyond the technical capabilities of the average hack. However, any sensitive data stored on a device (mobile or otherwise) presents some level of risk to you because no security approach is able to provide perfect protection; the goal is to use some simple and easy techniques to make compromising your data as difficult as possible.

Finding Macs

If you use a Mac, you might want to be able to locate it. Although the need for this is more obvious for a Mac laptop, it could potentially be useful if a desktop unexpectedly changes locations.

Enabling Find My Mac

To enable Find My Mac, perform the following steps:

1. Open the iCloud pane of the System Preferences application.

2. Check the **Find My Mac** check box.

3. Click **Allow** at the prompt. You can locate your Mac via the Find My iPhone application on your iCloud website or by using the Find My iPhone app on an iOS device.

Finding a Mac

To locate a Mac, perform the following steps:

1. Log into your iCloud website (see Lesson 1 for the details).

2. Click the **Application Switcher** button.

3. Click **Find My iPhone**. (This is labeled Find My iPhone no matter which device you are locating.) All the devices for which you have enabled the Find My Device feature under your iCloud are shown on the My Devices list. If a device is online and has been located, it is marked with a green dot.

4. Select the **Mac** you want to locate. The Mac's current location is shown on the map.

5. Click the **Info** (i) button. You see the Info dialog box, as shown in Figure 13.7.

FIGURE 13.7   A Mac has been found!

When you locate a Mac, you can send a message or play a sound, lock it, or wipe it. These work similarly to doing them for an iOS device. See the section, "Using Find My iPhone with iOS Devices," for the details.

Summary

In this lesson, you learned how to use iCloud to protect your devices. In the next lesson, you learn how to back up and restore your devices.

LESSON 14

Using iCloud to Back Up and Restore Devices

In this lesson, you learn how to protect the data on your iOS devices by backing them up. You also learn how to restore a device from your backup and how to manage your iCloud storage space.

Backing Up iOS Devices

Your iOS devices have lots of data on them, such as photos you've taken, contacts, apps, Home screen customizations, and so on. Although it's likely you have some of this data stored elsewhere (for example, your contacts are probably also stored on a computer), it would be a nuisance to have to redo your iOS device's configuration should something happen to it. In some cases, such as photos you've just taken, data may only be stored on the device for a period of time. By backing up your iOS device, you can easily restore it to recover your data and customized configuration when you need to.

Understanding Back Up Options

When it comes to backing up your iOS device, you have the following two options:

▶ **On your computer.** You can choose to store your backup data on the computer with which you sync the device using iTunes. There aren't many benefits to this option, but it does save space in the cloud if you store lots of other data there. However, this option has a number of disadvantages. Backups happen only when you sync the device to iTunes, so your backup is only as current as the most recent sync. Also, your backup is associated with a specific computer; should something happen to that computer, your backup could be lost.

▸ **On the cloud.** You can store your backup on the cloud. This has a number of benefits. The most important is that backups can happen any time a device has access to the Internet; you aren't limited to syncing with a specific computer as you are when you backup there. For example, if you are traveling with only your iOS device, you can still back it up. Because this is the best option for most people (and since this just happens to be a book on iCloud), using iCloud for your backups is the focus of this lesson.

Configuring How an iOS Device Is Backed Up

You can determine where an iOS device is backed up either via iTunes or on the device itself.

To set your backup location with iTunes, perform the following steps:

1. Connect the device to your computer and launch iTunes if it isn't open already.

2. Select the **device** on the Source list.

3. Click the **Summary** tab.

4. Click **Back up to iCloud**, as shown in Figure 14.1.

5. Click **Apply**. The device is synced according to the current settings and is backed up to your cloud.

To configure a back up location directly on the device, follow these steps:

1. Open the Settings app.

2. Tap **iCloud**.

3. Tap **Storage & Backup**.

FIGURE 14.1 You can determine the backup location for an iOS device using iTunes.

4. Set the **iCloud Backup** switch to the ON position, as shown in Figure 14.2. Your device is backed up the next time you sync with iTunes or perform a manual backup (explained in the next section).

Backing Up an iOS Device

An iOS device is automatically backed up when you sync it (via a USB cable) and when it is connected to a power source, locked, and connected to a Wi-Fi network. As long as these conditions are met regularly, the back up is maintained just as regularly.

To manually backup an iOS device, do either of the following:

▶ Connect the device to the computer with which it is synced. As part of the automatic sync process, the device is backed up.

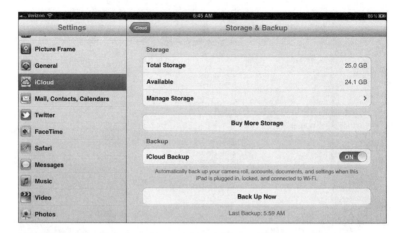

FIGURE 14.2   You can use the Settings app to determine where an iOS device is backed up.

▶ On the device, open the Settings app and tap **iCloud**. Tap **Storage & Backup**. Then tap **Back Up Now**, as shown in Figure 14.3. The device is backed up and synced. The progress of the backup is shown on the screen; you can use the device for other tasks while it is being backed up. The amount of time the process takes depends on the amount of data that needs to be backed up.

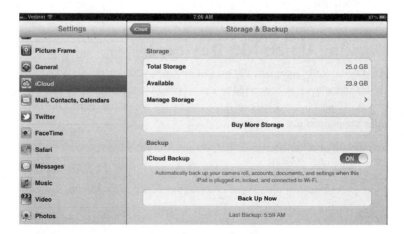

FIGURE 14.3   Tap Back Up Now to back up to the cloud.

CAUTION: **No Back Up When Wi-Fi Syncing**

When you sync a device over a Wi-Fi network, a backup is not included as it is when you sync a device by connecting it to a computer. To back up, you must sync the device over a cable or perform a manual back up using the **Back Up Now** button.

Restoring iOS Devices from a Backup

If you never have any problems with an iOS device or never have the need to restore it for any other reason, you don't need the information in this section. (If only life were that good!) However, you might at some point (actually rarely) need to restore an iOS device to solve a problem you are experiencing. As part of the restore process, you can choose to restore from your backup so that when the device is restored, it is in exactly the same state as it was when the backup was last performed (minus any problems you were experiencing, hopefully).

CAUTION: **Avoid Data Loss**

When you restore an iOS device, all its data is erased. If you don't have data backed up, it is lost when the restore occurs. In almost all cases, the backup is refreshed before the restore process starts. However, if that doesn't happen for some reason, perform a manual backup (if you can) before restoring the device.

To restore a device from your backup, perform the following steps:

1. Connect the device to the computer with which it is synced.

2. Click the **Summary** tab. A sync is performed, which includes backing up the device. Let this process finish before you move onto the next step. (You know the process is complete when the sync information disappears from the Information pane at the top of the iTunes window).

3. Click the **Restore** button.

4. Click **Restore** or **Restore and Update** (if there are software updates available). The current version of the iOS software is downloaded to the computer (if it hasn't already been downloaded, which happens automatically when iTunes finds an update) and extracted. The restore process begins. During the restore process, you see various status changes in iTunes (such as the device disappearing from iTunes for a time) along with screen changes on the device, such as the Connect to iTunes or software install progress. You don't need to take any action during this time; iTunes prompts you when your action is required. You can use the computer (including iTunes) for other tasks during this process. Some prompts are informational; click **OK** to close them or just ignore them, and they clear in around ten seconds. When the software installation process is complete, you see the Set Up screen, as shown in Figure 14.4.

FIGURE 14.4   Use the Set Up screen to choose to restore a device from your backup.

5. Ensure the **Restore from the backup of** radio button is selected (it is the default).

6. If you don't want to restore from the most recent backup for some reason, select the version of the backup you do want to restore from on the menu. It is rare to restore from something other than the most recent backup, but you do have that option available to you.

7. Click **Continue**. Data from your backup is copied onto the device. This includes all your settings (such as syncs, Home

screen customization, and so on), photos you've taken on the device, and so on. As the process continues, you see its progress in the restore progress window. When the process is complete, a dialog appears informing you of this. You can ignore it or click **OK** to clear it. The device restarts and is synced. When the sync finishes, the device should be in the same configuration and have the same data as it did as of the time and date of the most recent backup (or as of the time and date of an earlier backup if you selected one in step 6).

TIP: **When Did I Back Up?**

You can see the data and time of your most recent backup in a couple of places. When a device is connected to iTunes (using a cable or over a Wi-Fi network), open the Summary tab and look at the time and date at the bottom of the Backup section. Or open the Storage & Backup screen on the device; the date and time of the most recent backup is shown just below the Back Up Now button.

Managing Your iCloud Storage Space

Your iCloud account includes 5GB of online storage space by default. This space is used to store a number of things including: email, documents, your iOS device backups, and so on. Music, apps, books, and other content you purchase from the iTunes Store or music you are storing on the cloud, via iTunes Match, does not count against your storage space.

To see how your space is being used, open the Settings app, tap **iCloud**, and then tap **Storage & Backup**. In the Storage section, you see the total storage space for your iCloud account and the amount of space that is available. If you don't store a lot of documents on your devices, it's likely that the 5GB of space is sufficient for you; it is plenty for your backups.

If you are nearing the limit of your space (the available amount is small), you can remove data by tapping Manage Storage and deleting items you don't need any more, which frees up space for your account. More information about managing your online storage space is provided in Lesson 1, "Getting Started with Your iCloud Account and Website."

Summary

In this lesson, you learned how to protect the data on your iOS devices by backing them up; you also learned how to restore a device from your backup and how to manage your iCloud storage space.

Index

T

Sams**TeachYourself**

from Sams Publishing

Sams **Teach Yourself in 10 Minutes**
offers straightforward, practical answers
for fast results.

These small books of 250 pages or less
offer tips that point out shortcuts and
solutions, cautions that help you avoid
common pitfalls, and notes that explain
additional concepts and provide additional
information. By working through the
10-minute lessons, you learn everything
you need to know quickly and easily!

When you only have time for the answers,
Sams Teach Yourself books are your
best solution.

Visit **informit.com/samsteachyourself**
for a complete listing of the products
available.

Safari
Books Online

FREE
Online Edition

Your purchase of **Sams Teach Yourself iCloud in 10 Minutes** includes access to a free online edition for 45 days through the **Safari Books Online** subscription service. Nearly every Sams book is available online through **Safari Books Online**, along with thousands of books and videos from publishers such as Addison-Wesley Professional, Cisco Press, Exam Cram, IBM Press, O'Reilly Media, Prentice Hall, Que, and VMware Press.

Safari Books Online is a digital library providing searchable, on-demand access to thousands of technology, digital media, and professional development books and videos from leading publishers. With one monthly or yearly subscription price, you get unlimited access to learning tools and information on topics including mobile app and software development, tips and tricks on using your favorite gadgets, networking, project management, graphic design, and much more.

Activate your FREE Online Edition at
informit.com/safarifree

STEP 1:   Enter the coupon code: ARHYKCB.

STEP 2:   New Safari users, complete the brief registration form.
Safari subscribers, just log in.

If you have difficulty registering on Safari or accessing the online edition,
please e-mail customer-service@safaribooksonline.com